D0790108

THE PELICAN GUIDE TO
the Shenandoah

Blue Ridge Parkway

THE PELICAN GUIDE TO
the Shenandoah

With Sidetrips to Charlottesville and the Alleghenys

REGINA H. PIERCE
and SHARON G. YACKSO

Pelican Publishing Company
GRETNA 1987

Information in this guidebook is based on authoritative data available at the time of printing. Prices and hours of operation of businesses listed are subject to change without notice. Readers are asked to take this into account when consulting this guide.

Library of Congress Cataloging-in-Publication Data

Pierce, Regina H.
  The Pelican guide to the Shenandoah.

  Includes index.
    1. Shenandoah River Valley (Va. and W. Va.)—,
Description and travel—Guide-books. 2. Charlottesville
(Va.)—Description—Guide-books. 3. Allegheny
Mountains—Description and travel—Guide-books.
I. Yackso, Sharon G. II. Title.
F232.S5P53   1987   917.5.5'90443   87-6984
ISBN: 0-88289-652-0

All photos courtesy of Virginia Division of Tourism, 202
North Ninth Street, Suite 500, Richmond, VA 23219

Published by Pelican Publishing Company, Inc.
1101 Monroe Street, Gretna, Louisiana 70053
Manufactured in the United States of America

Many thanks to
Rachel Garfield and Valerie Marini
for special assistance.

Shenandoah River

Contents

List of Maps

THE PELICAN GUIDE TO
the Shenandoah

The Natural Bridge

1
How To Use This Guide

The guide begins at the Harpers Ferry National Historic Park. It takes the reader "up the Valley" to Lexington, stopping along the way at both the heavily touristed sites and the quieter towns. Sidetrips to the more cosmopolitan Charlottesville area and the remote counties of Highland and Bath have been added because of their proximity, historical significance, and natural beauty.

There are five territories that offer more to see and do than some of their neighbors. For the convenience of the reader, the chapters on these places are divided into sub-sections, such as **Dining** and **Places to Visit**. Chapters on the other counties, towns, and scenic highways begin with a brief history and introduction before going on to describe the points of interest.

The purpose of this guide is to give a feeling about the nature of each community and a description of its unique sights and services; consequently, only the more unusual or singular places to visit, eat, or stay have been included. Listings of the chain restaurants or motels can be found by consulting either the Chamber of Commerce or the local telephone book.

Unless otherwise designated, prices generally fall into the moderate range. Families on a budget can enjoy the beauty and history of the Valley as easily as resort vacationers, although as is usual, one can expect to pay more at a place with a fancier setting or more elaborate menu.

The Shenandoah Valley is continually growing and many fine businesses are opening their doors to visitors. Those traveling through the Valley of Virginia are encouraged to read the local newspapers and talk with residents to be sure not to miss anything new.

2

The Shenandoah Valley: A Short History

Shenandoah, Daughter of the Stars, was named by the Indians. The Valley, bounded to the east by the soft Blue Ridge Mountains and to the west by the more jagged Allegheny Mountains, was so plentiful in game and fish that it was reserved as a common hunting ground for the early tribes of the region.

Traditionally, the Valley begins at Harpers Ferry, where the Shenandoah and Potomac rivers join. It ends just below Lexington at a rise, where smaller rivers create the Shenandoah River. These geographic boundaries of the Valley, however, have become blurred through the years. Towns as far as fifty miles away often include themselves within the Shenandoah. Since the Valley follows the northward flowing Shenandoah River, going "up the Valley" has always meant traveling south.

The settlement at Jamestown had been thriving for almost a hundred years before the first pioneers entered the Valley of Virginia. The Blue Ridge marked the beginning of wilderness for these easterners and few were anxious to explore the territory beyond. When the first settlers arrived near Harrisonburg, however, they found the Valley as rich as the American natives had described. Soon, homesteads were built, relatives

13

Shenandoah Valley

were sent for, and the Valley began to take on a new face. The majority of newcomers were Scotch-Irish and Germans, who had come to seek refuge from religious persecution. At first, these early residents lived and worked peacefully with the Indians. As time went on and more settlers moved in, however, disagreements began. Small skirmishes eventually developed into full-scale battles. No longer on friendly terms with the Indians, the pioneers had to build their homes strong enough to withstand attacks. Generals Washington and Wayne ordered the construction of forts, and eventually the Indians were expelled and held out of colonial territories by force.

The history of the Shenandoah can also be told through the actions of many of our national patriots, heroes, and explorers. As a young man, George Washington surveyed the Valley and even left his initials on one of the seven natural wonders of the world, which is located at the southern end. Thomas Jefferson, who lived just "over the mountain," came through the area often. During the Revolutionary War, he used Staunton as a temporary hideout. Patrick Henry, James Monroe, James Madison, and many others have left stories and bits of lore in many Valley towns.

The old buffalo trail that ran the length of the Valley was widened by horses and later by wagons. It became known as the Valley Pike, now U.S. 11. Many travelers used this byway as they migrated to the mid-West. Towns grew and prospered along this thoroughfare. The crossroads leading over the Alleghenys became busy centers, as state institutions and colleges were located nearby.

During the Civil War, Sheridan's order to burn the "bread-basket of the South" meant the destruction of most of the Valley's biggest farms. Battles were fought up and down the Shenandoah, ravaging some towns while leaving others barely touched.

The Civil War remains a fascinating period for history buffs. Many monuments, museums, and markers commemorating battles and heroes are to be seen throughout the Valley. It is not unusual when driving through the countryside to see collectors searching pastureland for the bullets, medals, and buttons that are still found hidden in the earth.

The Scotch-Irish and German settlers brought with them traditions of strong families, farming, and strict faith. The Valley became known for its old family roots, its productive farms, and the surprising number of its churches.

Throughout the years the almost exclusively agricultural base of the area has given way to include some small industries and factories. The opening of the Skyline Drive and the Blue Ridge Parkway along the crest of the mountains has brought many new visitors to the Valley to enjoy the changing leaves, underground caverns, and historical sites.

3

Harpers Ferry
National Historic Park

Harpers Ferry lies at the entrance of the Valley. Here the highway cuts through rolling hills and farms edged with bushy trees. The mountains abruptly come into view, guarding the grazing cows and seasonal crops. Very soon the motorist is in the hollows of the Blue Ridge. The farms that stretched back to the horizon are no longer visible. A rock hillside on the left and the Shenandoah River on the right usher in the road to Harpers Ferry National Historic Park.

The allure of Harpers Ferry goes beyond its picturesque setting at the confluence of the Shenandoah and Potomac rivers. The area's development has created a community which lives in two eras. The Park's restored buildings recreate the early eighteenth century: Smithies shape horseshoes and Union soldiers prop themselves against walls polishing guns, while visitors watch and ask questions. Just around the corner an avenue of modern shops, boutiques, and galleries tempts customers with more modern pleasures.

The best way to appreciate this spot in the northern Valley is to walk every square inch of it. The Park demonstrations are the mainstay attractions, but the small discoveries to be made along the way make Harpers Ferry a unique historical center.

History

Robert Harper was the first of many to capitalize on the water power of the area between the Shenandoah and Potomac rivers. He became the town's most important businessman in 1747 when he built a mill and took over a ferry service that later bore his name. Although industry blossomed around the mill, it was the federal government that became the dominating influence when George Washington proposed Harpers Ferry as the site of a national armory in the 1790s. Eventually, the armory supported businesses and locals could purchase their major goods at the company store.

Harpers Ferry thrived as a small pocket of industry until October 1859, when John Brown's raid forecast the Civil War, which followed seventeen months later. Brown was a self-appointed liberator of the slaves, and his small band of guerrillas attempted to seize the weapons safeguarded at the armory. The men were captured by Col. Robert E. Lee and Lt. J. E. B. Stuart after they had barricaded themselves in a building. When the war broke out, Harpers Ferry was almost destroyed. The arsenal was burned and troops from both sides fought bitterly over the occupation of the town.

The postbellum years brought about a physical restoration, but a series of floods in the late 1800s ended any hopes of a return to an industrial center. The only institution which did flourish was Storer College, a school for freed slaves sponsored by a New England philanthropist. It was the U.S. Government which once again took a hand in spurring the town back to prosperity. The National Park Service purchased and restored many of the original buildings. It now owns and operates the Harpers Ferry National Historic Park.

Places to Visit/Things to Do

Visitor Center (Shenandoah Street, across from parking area). This should be your first stop before viewing the historic area.

A slide show, several small exhibits, and the knowledgeable park attendants are all extremely helpful in planning a sightseeing day.

Harpers Ferry Historical Area. Many of the original buildings which once contained the businesses, shops, and offices of this busy industrial community have been restored by the National Park Service. In them, you may see a blacksmith in authentic dress pumping his bellows and other apprentice craftsmen practicing their trades. Visitors' questions are answered at length as workers temper metal or mind the general store. Free.

Jefferson Rock (follow footpath leading from St. Peter's Catholic Church). Turning left at the top of High Street, you will see a lane of large Victorian homes pointing toward the ruins of the Episcopal church. From there, a path leads up to Jefferson Rock, where two distinctive sights are found. Of historical value is the mountain view and river which Jefferson described as ". . . worth a trip across the Alantic." The other sight is the rock itself, which has been inscribed with thousands upon thousands of names and initials of individuals and romancing couples. Where time has worn and faded old initials, new ones have been freshly etched.

Storer College (Fillmore Street). The offices of the paymaster and clerks of the Harpers Ferry Armory were transformed into a college for newly freed slaves after the Civil War. When the College closed its doors in 1955, the National Park Service acquired the campus. The buildings are now on public display and are also used as a training center for Park employees.

High Street. Small shops sit just below street level. The original cobblestone street had to be constructed in "corduroy," a method of paving to create a series of small steps so that horses wouldn't lose their footing on the steep hill.

Shopping

The primary avenue for shopping is High Street. As can be expected in an historic area which caters to tourists, there are many souvenir stores. Civil War items occupy the majority of shelves, but each establishment singles itself out with specialty items such as jewelry or local crafts. Gift shops are also in abundance, with the country/Americana motif as the predominant theme. The antique stores are found along Potomac Street, which follows the railroad tracks.

To make certain that one's enthusiasm for shopping and sightseeing does not begin to wane, the stores with homemade cookies and candies or hot roasted peanuts are strategically located.

Dining

Up and down High Street, quaint cafes are neighbors to rustic carry-outs with menus of simple (and usually homemade) food. The warmer months bring diners of all ages to the many outdoor patios and porches. The area is also a culinary dream for children as eateries offering hot dogs, hamburgers, or ice cream abound.

For a more conventional meal, the locals all recommend the dining room at the Hilltop House Hotel (Ridge Street), especially the weekend buffets. The hotel has the comfortable feeling of an old Southern hotel. Spacious rooms with polished floors look out onto one of the best views in the area. For small-town activity, relax in comfortable porch rockers and enjoy the rock cliffs that shadow the passing river. Phone (304) 535-6302.

Another favorite of the residents, located outside of the historic district, is the dining room at the Cliffside Motor Inn (U.S. 340 North). The restaurant also offers a popular weekend buffet. Phone (304) 535-6321.

Lodging

Hilltop House Hotel. Travelers will appreciate the same hospitality which attracted Mark Twain and Woodrow Wilson: simple but comfortable accommodations, good food, and breathtaking views.

For information write: Hilltop House Hotel, Box 806, Harpers Ferry, WV 24456, or phone (304) 535-6321.

Countryside Bed and Breakfast. The owners have a well-established reputation for friendliness. The location near Harpers Ferry lends itself to either a quiet hike or a busy sightseeing day.

For information write: Countryside Bed and Breakfast, Lisa and Daniel Hileman, Box 57, Summit Point, WV 25446, or phone (304) 725-2614.

Recreation

Rafting and Canoeing. The area provides the ideal environment for a trip downstream. For information contact Blue Ridge Outfitters, P.O. Box 456, Harpers Ferry, WV 25425 (phone 725-3444) or River and Trail Outfitters, Box 246, Knoxville, MD (phone 695-5177).

Hiking. There are twelve miles of trails throughout the Harpers Ferry National Historic Park. Sections of the Appalachian Trail and the C. & O. Canal Park offer additional hiking. Harpers Ferry also houses the Appalachian Trail Headquarters. There are guidebooks, maps, and other sources of information for wanderers who wish to cover any of the approximately 2,000 miles from Maine to Georgia.

For information write: Appalachian Trail Headquarters, P.O. Box 807, Harpers Ferry, WV 25425, or phone (304) 535-6331. Open 9 to 5 Monday through Friday.

Fishing. Before tossing in the lures at any river in this tri-state area, call (304) 535-6371 to find out the necessary license requirements for the spot you've picked.

Rock Climbing. The variety of ascents at all levels of difficulty make this the best spot in the Valley for rock climbers. The Park requires all climbers to check in at the Ranger Station before starting out and up.

Seasonal Events

Mountain Heritage Arts and Crafts Festival (from U.S. 340 between Harpers Ferry and Charles Town, take Halltown exit and turn right on S.R. 230, follow signs to S.R. 220). Held in early June and late September, this is one of the largest and busiest of the many arts and crafts shows held in the Valley. Almost 200 craftspersons are on hand as Appalachian folk music and bluegrass bands provide a festive atmosphere. Admission charge. Phone toll-free 800-624-2577 or (304) 725-2055.

Old Tyme Christmas. Caroling, a living nativity, and special events for children put Harpers Ferry back into the nineteenth century for Christmas. First two weekends in December. Free.

For information write: Harpers Ferry Merchants Association, Harpers Ferry, WV 24456, or phone (304) 525-2482 or 535-2372.

Resources

Jefferson County Chamber of Commerce
Box 426
Charles Town, WV 25414
(304) 725-2055

4

Bolivar

Originally known as Mudfort, this village was named for Simon Bolivar, the famous liberator of five South American countries. No one seems to know exactly how the town derived its name, but it is conjectured that Bolivar's victories appeared quite frequently in the papers at about the same time the community was officially formed. Recently, a bust of Simon Bolivar was presented to the community by the president of Venezuela in appreciation of the recognition of that country's national hero. Several years ago, in honor of Simon Bolivar's birthday, ambassadors brought a colorful Latin American festival to the streets of this small West Virginia town.

Points of Interest

Primarily a residential community, Bolivar has only a few shops and businesses as compared with Harpers Ferry, its neighbor down the hill. Yet travelers should take at least an hour or so to walk the main avenue, Washington Street, where children still set up lemonade stands by tree-lined sidewalks, and small general stores are situated every couple of blocks. Along this main street Don Miller, an accomplished artisan, has a gallery and shop to display his fine, handwrought pieces of pewter. He and his wife are willing to stop and chat about the art of shaping pewter and about hometown history. Phone (301) 535-6508.

It is worth the time to dine in Bolivar, particularly if you want to escape the crowds in Harpers Ferry. Chianti's Restaurant and Garden Cafe (1270 Washington Street) creates a new menu daily. Its smaller bar area adjoins a spacious dining room with a Mexican touch. Phone (301) 535-6508.

5

Charles Town

Proud of its association with America's first presidential family, Charles Town was named for George Washington's younger brother, Charles. Col. Charles Washington laid out eighty acres of land in half-acre lots and donated the four center lots to the public. Samuel Washington owned a large estate on the outskirts of town which was designed by our first president. A number of homes built by descendants of the family can still be found within the city limits.

The story of the abolitionist John Brown is recorded in the *county courthouse* (Washington and George streets). Here he was tried and convicted of treason and conspiracy for his unsuccessful attempt to capture the munitions at Harpers Ferry and free the slaves. *The Jefferson County Museum* (200 E. Washington Street) displays artifacts from this incident along with a detailed account of the uprising.

Courthouse open 9 to 5 Monday through Friday, 9 to noon Saturday, year round. Phone (301) 725-9762. Museum open 10 to 4 Monday through Saturday, April to October. Free. Phone (301) 725-8628.

Points of Interest

The old brick buildings of present-day Charles Town now frame a busy downtown area. *The Old Opera House Theatre*

Company (204 N. George Street), once the home for traveling shows and vaudeville acts, currently stages a series of popular plays. Annual schedule of productions available on request. Phone (301) 725-4420. Open year round for viewing 9 to 5 Monday through Friday. Admission charge.

The Charles Town Races (on U.S. 340 North between Charles Town and Harpers Ferry), a thoroughbred track, offers a different kind of excitement. Since there is no legalized gambling in Virginia, busloads of spectators drive across the border for a night at the races. Grandstand tickets are nominally priced and instructions on betting are free. For information write: Charles Town Races, Group Sales/Special Events Dept., P.O. Box 551, Charles Town, WV 25414. Phone (304) 725-7001, toll-free from Washington area 800-737-2323, or toll-free from Baltimore area 800-685-0200. Nearby *Summit Point Raceway* (Summit Point Road) also advertises fast finishes for sports cars, motorcycles, and go-carts. Open mid-March to November. For information write: Summit Point Raceway, Summit Point Road, P.O. Box 190, Summit Point, WV 25446, or phone (304) 725-8444.

The Iron Rail Inn and Cellar Club (124 E. Washington Street) is the place for a leisurely dinner in an elegant restored home. Phone (304) 725-0052. Several small diners serving good home cooking are found on Washington Street, and *Granny's Kitchen* (N. Washington Street) is a good stop for pie and coffee. Phone (304) 725-1575.

Resources

Jefferson County Chamber of Commerce
200 E. Washington St.
P.O. Box 426
Charles Town, WV 25414
Tel. (304) 725-2055

6

Berryville
and Clarke County

Clarke County, named for the explorer George Rogers Clark, was originally settled by a select group of English aristocrats. Unlike the majority of pioneers who were seeking inexpensive land or religious freedom, these cavaliers came from the formal manors of eastern Virginia's Tidewater region. Although the members of this adventuresome group were eager to settle in relatively unexplored territory, they were not quite bold enough to venture into the heart of the Valley wilderness.

Berryville, the county seat of Clarke, was named for its founder, Benjamin Berry. It is best remembered for its lawless beginnings. Once called Battletown, its infamous tavern witnessed many evenings of ale drinking and fighting.

One lively character named Daniel Morgan was reputed to be the peacekeeper of the neighborhood. He was, nevertheless, frequently fined for misbehavior. It is told that he kept a supply of rocks along the roadside leading to his house so that he could stone pursuers if he had to flee home. When the French and Indian War began, Morgan joined in the effort to protect the American settlements; he was named Captain of Militia for his bravery. The Revolutionary War also called upon Morgan's skill. He and his riflemen were largely responsible for the American victory at Saratoga, which was a turning point in the long struggle for independence. For his bravery, he earned the title "Thunderbolt of War" as well as Congressional recognition. At Morgan's first home, "Soldiers Rest," young George Washington often stayed while he surveyed that region of the Valley.

By the onset of the Civil War, Clarke County was known as the richest grainbin of the South. Col. John Mosby was the legendary Confederate figure often seen raiding General Sheridan's troops behind the Union lines. When six of his cavalrymen, known as Mosby's Rangers, were captured and hanged by Sheridan's command, Mosby retaliated. Here in the county he hanged six Union troopers with a message to Sheridan that two more would die for every Confederate soldier hanged in the future. This ended the senseless killings.

Points of Interest

In downtown Berryville, the buildings are of turn-of-the-century architecture. The parking meters still take pennies and the variety store uses an old-time money-changer which clangs back and forth along a pulley between the cashier and the second floor office. *The Clarke County Museum* (104 N. Church Street) houses historical artifacts of the region. Free. Phone (703) 955-2600.

Berryville offers two enjoyable restaurants from which to choose. *The Lighthouse Restaurant* (13 E. Main Street) is an upstairs dining room which specializes in fresh seafood entrees. Phone (703) 955-1301. *The Meeting Place* (113 E. Main Street) is more informal and has a long menu, ranging from soup and sandwiches to sole florentine. Phone (703) 955-2200.

The surrounding county claims to be "Virginia's Best Kept Secret." The aristocratic influence of its early settlers is still felt. Many large estates grace the hillsides and the English tradition of fox-hunting continues. The Chamber of Commerce distributes a brochure entitled "We Welcome You to Clarke County," listing historical manors and churches that are open to the public. For this brochure write: Berryville-Clarke County Chamber of Commerce, 5 South St., Berryville, VA 22611, or phone (703) 955-4200. Of special interest is *Old Chapel Episcopal Church,* the oldest place of worship west of the Blue Ridge Mountains.

In Millwood, the *Burwell-Morgan Mill* continues to grind wheat by its 200-year-old method. Originally owned by Daniel Morgan and Nathaniel Burwell, the mill sold its products to both armies during the Civil War. Open 9:30 to 4:30 daily except Thursday, May to October. Admission charge. Phone (703) 837-1799. Also in Millwood is the *Old Time Blacksmith Shop,* once a wayside where ale and spirits were sold. Free.

In nearby Boyce is the *Blandy Experimental Farm* (on U.S. 340 between Berryville and White Post) of the University of Viginia. Its arboretum, housing more than 5,000 plants, is open to the public. Open daily from sunrise to sunset. Free. Phone (703) 837-1758.

The little village of *White Post* is named for the marker erected by George Washington that points the direction to Lord Fairfax's home. The village itself is listed on the National Register of Historic Places. One of its more unusual business establishments, *White Post Restorations,* (SR 658) is a world leader in refurbishing antique cars. With space for sixty vehicles, the showroom has a fascinating collection of "motor cars" on display. Free. Phone (703) 837-1140.

Also in White Post is *L'Auberge Provençale,* a country inn hosted in Old World style. Although the meals and lodging are more expensive than the usual Valley prices, the fourth-generation French chef prepares gourmet dishes such as fresh roasted squab with truffles. Dining rooms open 6 P.M. to 10:30 P.M. daily except Tuesday. Sunday dinner 4 P.M. to 9 P.M. Restaurant closed from January 1 to mid-February; inn rooms open year round. For reservations write: L'Auberge Provençale, P.O. Box 119, White Post, VA 22663, or phone (703) 837-1375.

Three noteworthy seasonal events are the *Antique Steam Engine Show* (admission charge), *Berryville Days* (a free community celebration), and the *Blue Ridge Hunt Point-to-Point Races* (admission charge). This steeplechase draws spectators from the surrounding "horse country" as well as the Washington, D.C. area. The horse racing, the people-watching, and the picnicking are all entertaining.

7

Winchester and Frederick County

Known as the "apple capital," Winchester has at its center broad, tree-lined streets, gracious homes, and pre-Civil War buildings. Encircling this inner ring are large shopping malls, hotels, and factories. Frederick County is also the home for many businesses, but apple orchards and small villages make up most of the countryside.

Visitors will find that the residents are eager to share a bit of Winchester's history. Stopping to ask directions, the newcomer may also be told how the city changed hands seventy-two times during the Civil War. The number of restored historic sites is evidence of the community's commitment to the preservation of its heritage.

History

The Shawnee Indians are credited as the founding fathers of Winchester and Frederick County. They were often drawn to a campsite next to a clear spring, which still flows today. Their legend claims, "He who drinks of this water will soon return."

In the 1730s, Abraham Hollingsworth was also attracted to this spring. He purchased 582 acres of the surrounding land and began a settlement at what must then have seemed the

Virginia apple blossoms in springtime

edge of the world. Col. James Wood laid out the streets for a village and it was called Fredericktown.

Wood later donated land to enlarge the boundaries. A more famous and colorful resident, Thomas Lord Fairfax, also granted large portions of his holdings to the county. A history of disagreements with his mother and grandmother and a broken engagement left Fairfax a resolute bachelor who allowed no women into his home, "Greenway Court." He dressed in the finest English silks and satins and entertained his male companions until the age of ninety-one. He brought George Washington to the Valley to survey the lands west of the Blue Ridge. Despite Fairfax's lifelong loyalty to the British, the two remained close friends.

Three short years before the outbreak of the French and Indian War, Fredericktown was officially recognized and named Winchester at Wood's request, in memory of his hometown in England. The ensuing uprising provided George Washington with his first military command. He traveled to Fort Duquesne with the English General Braddock.

After Braddock's defeat, Washington returned to Winchester, where the settlers desperately needed protection. Very little money was designated by the House of Burgesses to erect a fort, so Washington imported his own blacksmiths from Mount Vernon to defray the cost of building what was to become Fort Loudoun.

The Revolutionary War brought to the forefront another military hero, Gen. Daniel Morgan. Morgan was placed in charge of Hessian prisoners, but the Continental army failed to give him the provisions for their care. He wisely put them to work planting many of the first apple orchards and caring for the trees in exchange for their keep.

Winchester was again destined to become a hub of activity during a major conflict. The city changed hands no less than seventy-two times during the Civil War. Stonewall Jackson and Philip Sheridan had headquarters here, while more than one hundred clashes took place in an effort to protect the food-producing Shenandoah Valley.

Winchester's struggles continued with post-war reconstruction. The mild climate, canals, and railroads eventually turned the area into an agricultural and industrial center. Winchester's modern history embraces the town's own Tom, Dick, and Harry—the three Byrd brothers. Tom established his name as a planter and orchardist, Richard is known for his expeditions to the Poles, and Harry was a governor and senator for his state.

Places to Visit/Things to Do

Abram's Delight (1340 Pleasant Valley Road). Abraham Hollingsworth, one of the area's first settlers, built his house on the site of a Shawnee Indian camp. After completing the working buildings, he brought his family to the Valley and their new home. "A delight to behold" was how Hollingsworth described his estate. The house now open to visitors was built by his son Isaac.

Open 10 to 5 daily, April to October. Admission charge. Phone 662-6519.

Stonewall Jackson Headquarters (415 N. Braddock Street). General Jackson's Civil War campaign was orchestrated from the home of Lt. Col. Lewis T. Moore. It became known as his Upper Valley Headquarters.

Open 10 to 5 daily, April 1 to October. Admission charge. Phone 667-3242.

George Washington's Office Museum (Cork and Braddock streets). While serving in the Virginia militia, Washington used this small log cabin as his office. At this time, his major responsibility was the protection of Winchester's borders, which were vulnerable to Indian attacks. After a year and a half in these tight quarters he relocated to Fort Loudoun. This original office was later made into a home and eventually a town hall.

Open 10 to 5, April 1 to October. Admission charge. Phone 662-4412.

Belle Grove (1 mile south of Middletown, on U.S. 11). As a property of the National Trust for Historic Preservation, this eighteenth century working plantation focuses on the folk heritage of the Northern Shenandoah Valley. It is open to the public for guided tours and special events; thousands of visitors come annually.

Open 10 to 4 Monday through Saturday, 1 to 5 Sunday, April through October. Admission charge.

Preservation and Quilt Shops are open daily year round, and the special holiday shop opens late in November. Phone 869-2028. (See also **Seasonal Events**.)

Sheridan's Headquarters (corner of Piccadilly and Braddock streets). Sheridan was using this home as he headed down the Valley Pike to the Battle of Cedar Creek. Here he inspired his retreating army into driving off the Confederate troops. This landmark is easily located; Winchester's symbol of a giant apple stands outside. However, the interior of the home is not open to the public.

Office and fort used by George Washington in Winchester

Wayside Theatre. Diverse plays are professionally presented in the summer. Visitors can take in the small village of Middletown before watching the show.

For information write: Wayside Theatre, Middletown, VA 22645, or phone (703) 869-1776 (box office) or 869-1782 (administration office).

Shenandoah College and Conservatory (Millwood Pike). A monthly calendar of plays and musical events is offered. Nationally known musicians are featured each season. Admission charge. Phone 665-4500.

Shopping

Although Winchester has several large malls, some of the more interesting stores are found in and around the Loudoun

Street Mall, a pedestrian walkway that has always been downtown. The only holdover from earlier days is Anderson's grocery store, where the screen door still slaps behind a customer stopping in for a wedge of cheese and the local news. A piece of history is offered here for free—the walls are covered with the pictures of former residents and their newsworthy moments.

Also on Loudoun Street are several small shops offering gourmet foods and kitchen conveniences. Many antique and other specialty shops are to be found on the side streets. *The Handworks Gallery and Stained Glass Studio* (20 W. Boscowan Street) specializes in small gifts crafted by artisans. Phone 662-3927. *The Colonial Art and Craft Shop* (25 W. Piccadilly) has an extensive inventory of fine home and gift items. Phone 662-6513. An uplifting final stop on any shopping tour is *Party Time* (38 E. Piccadilly), where confetti, streamers, harlequin masks, and gag gifts are available for all manner of celebrations. Phone 667-2046.

Dining

The Wayside Inn in Middletown (773 Main Street) is the choice for a special evening out. The Americana decor in each of the dining rooms, ranging from pub-style to elegant, is truly reminiscent of the eighteenth century. The colonial cooking, served by waitresses in long dresses, is in keeping with the traditional atmosphere. Diners should allow time to walk around the Inn to appreciate the antiques and paintings. Phone 869-1797.

There are several alternatives for more casual dining. *Cafe Sofia* (688 N. Loudoun Street) caters to seafood lovers, and on Tuesday nights Bulgarian cuisine can be sampled. Phone 667-2950. *Manuel's and Wife* (Holiday Inn, U.S. 11 South) is a steak and seafood restaurant with a relaxed, country setting. Phone 662-1192.

For simple, homecooked meals or a "blue plate special," one of the many diners should be considered. Some are flashy with bright neon signs, while others are simply a long tunnel in the side of a building.

Lodging

Wayside Inn. Travelers passing through the Valley have stopped here for over 188 years. The interior appears as though the eighteenth century visitors had just stepped out for a moment. The food is wonderful and the antiques are exceptional. (See also **Dining.**)

For information write: Wayside Inn, 773 Main Street, Middletown, VA 22645, or phone (703) 869-1797.

Recreation

Clearbrook Park (6 miles north of Winchester on U.S. 11 and SR 672) and *Sherando Park* (2 miles east of Stephens City on VA 277). Frederick County supports both facilities. Each park has a lake, picnic shelters, and ball diamonds. Clearbrook has twenty acres of open space, while Sherando has forty acres, including self-guided nature trails.

Clearbrook Park open 9 A.M. to dusk April 1 to October 31. Sherando Park open 9 A.M. to dusk year round. Free.

Seasonal Events

Apple Blossom Festival. The Valley celebrates spring with this annual festival dedicated to a delicate pink flower. Parades, queens, and "Sunday in the Park" with apple crate derbies, arts and crafts displays, and mock Civil War battles end four days of fun.

Early May. Admission charge to some events. For information write: Apple Blossom Festival, P.O. Box 3099, Winchester, VA 22601.

Belle Grove. This plantation's list of special events begins in April and ends with its Christmas tours. Special highlights are the quilt exhibition in October and Draft Horse and Mule Day held around Labor Day. (See also **Places to Visit.**) Admission charge. For information write: Belle Grove, Inc., P.O. Box 137, Middletown, VA 22645, or phone (703) 869-2028.

Sherando Festival (Sherando Park, Stevens City). Sheepherding exhibits, barbecues, and country music have made this day a family favorite. The county Olympics have competitions for all ages and the fireworks end the day with a splash. Mid-June. Free. For information call (703) 667-4607.

Resources

Winchester-Frederick County Chamber of Commerce
2 North Cameron Street
Winchester, VA 22601
(703) 662-4118

Preservation of Historic Winchester
8 E. Cork St.
Winchester, VA 22601
(703) 667-3577

This non-profit organization can supply free information on Winchester's history and architecture as well as brochures describing walking tours.

Virginia State Travel Service
P.O. Box 38
Clearbrook, VA 22624
(703) 667-0758

Travel service will supply free travel literature and maps of Virginia. Located on I-81 between exits 82 and 83, 6 miles north of Winchester.

8

Shenandoah County

The settlement of Shenandoah County was influenced by two of Virginia's great patrons, Lord Fairfax and George Washington. In 1752, Fairfax gave Jacob Miller enough land to lay out a town in this county, originally called Dunmore. Under the sponsorship of George Washington, then a member of the House of Burgesses, this new town was granted a charter in 1761 and named Woodstock. Washington was certainly familiar with the territory, since he had surveyed it in his youth and later defended it against Indian attacks.

At the onset of the Revolutionary War, Reverend Peter Muhlenberg instantly organized the Eighth Virginia Regiment. At the close of his Sunday sermon, Muhlenberg read from Ecclesiastes 3:18 ". . . there is a time to every purpose under heaven . . . a time for war and a time for peace." There at the pulpit he threw down his minister's garb and revealed the proud uniform of a Continental soldier. Muhlenberg was eventually promoted to the rank of general and worked closely with Washington throughout the war.

Another dramatic episode in this county's history occurred during the Civil War, when the "boy soldiers" of the Virginia Military Institute were initiated at the Battle of New Market. In a desperate move to halt the advancing Union troops of Gen.

Franz Sigel, Gen. John Breckenridge pulled 247 teen-aged cadets from their barracks at VMI. As the battle progressed and the casualties mounted, the teen-agers were sent to the front line and returned home victorious.

Today, Shenandoah County is a long and narrow section of the scenic valley for which it was eventually renamed. As one drives past rugged Massanutten Mountain or wide stretches of the Shenandoah River, small towns seem to pop up and then quickly disappear. Here the traveler can find many good reasons to slow down, take in the sights, and enjoy the recreation and lodging offered by these hospitable communities.

Points of Interest

Strasburg is best known for its annual summer presentations of the *Passion Play*. The American version of the original from Oberammergau, Germany is held in an outdoor garden amphitheater. 8:30 P.M. nightly except Sunday and Monday, July 5 to Labor Day. Write: Passion Play, Hwy. 11—Garden Amphitheatre, Strasburg, VA 22657, or phone (703) 465-3688. The town also sponsors the *Strasburg Museum* (King Street), a former railroad depot that tells the history of the craftsmanship once seen in farming communities. Open 10 to 4 May to October. Admission charge. *Hotel Strasburg* is a turn-of-the-century hospital and models itself after a country inn. For information write: Hotel Strasburg, 201 Holiday Street, Strasburg, VA 22657 or phone (703) 465-9191.

Traveling south on the Pike (U.S. 11) to Mt. Jackson, one finds two well-known lodges available at nearby Basye. *Bryce Resort* (follow VA 263 from exit 69 on I-81) caters to sportsmen, with windsurfing and grass skiing added to the usual golf, swimming, and tennis. Admission charge. For information write: Bryce Resort, P.O. Box 3, Bayse, VA 22810, or phone (703) 856-2181. *Sky Chalet* (take exit 69 on I-81, then go approximately 10 miles on VA 263) is a country inn on top of

Super Lick Ridge, where the view reaches across the mountains to West Virginia. An evening by the fireplace and a country meal with homemade bread is welcome after a day of hiking or horseback riding. For information write: Sky Chalet Country Inn, Star Route, Box 28, Mt. Jackson, VA 22842, or phone (703) 856-2147.

Woodstock continues to serve as the county seat. Of note are its courthouse (built from one of Thomas Jefferson's designs) and a tower erected on Massanutten Mountain. Located four miles from the city, the tower overlooks seventy miles of the Valley and seven bends of the Shenandoah River.

The biggest attraction in the county is the *Civil War Battlefield Park* (take exit 67 on I-81) in New Market. Here in this 160-acre park is the Hall of Valor, a memorial which depicts the course of the war through films and exhibits. Open daily 9 to 5. Admission charge. Write New Market Battlefield Park, Box 1864, New Market, VA 22844, or phone (703) 740-3102. *The Bushong farmhouse,* caught in the midst of the Battle of New Market, still stands. Walking paths lead to high bluffs above the Shenandoah River where the "boy soldiers" earned their place in history. Open 10 to 4 June 15 to Labor Day. Admission charge.

Nearby are two caverns, *Endless and Shenandoah Caverns.* The Endless Caverns were discovered by two boys chasing a rabbit, and an end to the many corridors has yet to be discovered. Shenandoah Caverns are known for their wide subterranean openings that are reached by elevators. Open daily, 9 to 5 winter, 9 to 6 spring and fall, 9 to 7 summer. Closed Christmas Day. Admission charge.

The town of New Market is well equipped for its many visitors. Authentic cooking from below the Mason-Dixon line is served in abundance at the *Southern Kitchen.* Overnight lodging which is centrally located can be found at the *Shenvalee* (take exit 67 from I-81; follow signs for 1 mile). From this quiet lodge many sightseeing and recreational activities are easily reached. Golf packages for the eighteen-hole P.G.A. course are available. For information write: Shenvalee, P.O. Box 430, New Market, VA 22844 or phone (703) 740-3181.

A popular seasonal event in the county is the *Shenandoah Valley Music Festival*. Each year, in late July or early September, the festival invites famous musicians for performances. Guest performances from orchestras to vocalists or big bands make up the schedule. Admission charge. For information write: Shenandoah Valley Music Festival, P.O. Box 12, Woodstock, VA 22664. The festival is held at the Orkney Springs Hotel, a part of the ShrineMont Conference Center (take exit 69 on I-81 and follow VA 263 to Orkney Springs), which is listed on the National Register of Historic Landmarks. Even when the festival is not under way, the hotel, with its absence of televisions and phones, is a charming place to stay. Parts of the building date back to the Civil War and the meals are served "family style." For information write: ShrineMont, Orkney Springs, VA 22845 or phone (703) 856-2141.

Resources

Mount Jackson Area Chamber of Commerce
Mount Jackson, VA 22842
(703) 477-3275

Woodstock Chamber of Commerce
113 N. Main St. Woodstock, VA 22664
(703) 459-2542

9

Front Royal
and Warren County

The origins of Front Royal are similar to those of many valley communities. The intersections of popular footpaths became crossroads of well-used byways, where enterprising merchants set up taverns and stores to serve the converging travelers. Settlements emerged as trade increased, attracting more businesses and families.

The wayside which was to become Front Royal distinguished itself by its rowdy behavior and nightly shootings, earning the name of "Helltown." The more dignified citizens, however, preferred to use Lehewtown, after the founder, Peter Lehew. The name Front Royal evolved in 1778 when a frustrated drill sergeant was directing his troops in the public square, where a large oak (emblem of English royalty) stood. When he failed to coax the correct maneuvers out of his recruits, he cried as a last resort, "Front the Royal Oak!"

By 1836, Front Royal was the county seat of Warren County. The town prospered as a wagon manufacturing center, drawing customers from the Southern and Western states. When the railroad entered the Valley in 1854, the first train made its long-awaited appearance in Front Royal.

As the War Between the States raged through the Valley, Front Royal and Warren County acquired an even more noteworthy reputation. On May 23, 1862, Stonewall Jackson started his famous valley campaign at the Battle of Front Royal. Mosby's Rangers also brought fame to the area through their ongoing clashes with Sheridan's Yankee troops. They managed to cut through Sheridan's entire cavalry when it was camped in the county.

Front Royal also served as the hideaway for the famous Civil War spy Belle Boyd. After shooting a Federal officer for trying to raise the United States flag over her West Virginia home, she came to help care for wounded Confederate soldiers. Tales of how Belle charmed Union officers for their secrets and how she dashed in and out of enemy lines to carry messages to General Jackson and her scandalous trial as a spy have been told again and again. Ironically, she fell in love with a Union lieutenant who overtook her ship as she was trying to escape to England. The two eventually married in London, but Belle's handsome husband was charged with desertion when he returned home and was sent to prison. Once again her beauty and courage triumphed, and he was released to live happier post-war years.

By the end of the 1800s the city and county had recovered from the war. In the early 1930s Congressional approval of the building of the Skyline Drive was a milestone in the area's development. Front Royal and Warren County now serve as the gateway to the Shenandoah National Park and its famous highway, the Skyline Drive.

Points of Interest

Although Front Royal and Warren County are best known for their proximity to the Skyline Drive, there are some additional attractions to see first.

The Skyline Caverns (by the intersection of I-81 and I-64) are the only place in the world where anthodites, the "orchids of the mineral kingdom," are able to grow. Open daily 8:30 to

6:30 during summer season, 9 to 4:30 November to Easter, 9 to 5:30 Labor Day to October and Easter to Memorial Day. Free. Write: Skyline Caverns, Inc., Box 193, Front Royal, VA 22630, or phone (703) 635-4545.

The eighty-six-acre *Thunderbird Museum and Archeological Park* (from U.S. 340, 7 miles south of Front Royal, take SR 737 west to Park entrance) follows 12,000 years of human history, beginning with exhibitions of arrowheads and early Indian tools to displays explaining how man adapts to a changing environment. Open 10 to 5 daily, mid-March through mid-November. Admission charge. Write: Thunderbird Museum, Rt. 1, Box 1375, Front Royal, VA 22630, or phone (703) 635-7337 or 635-3860.

In Front Royal itself, Civil War historians will want to stop in at the *Confederate Museum* (95 Chester Street) to see exhibits of the legendary heroes generals Jackson and Lee, Belle Boyd, and Mosby's Rangers.

Open weekdays 9 to 5, Sundays noon to 5, April 15 to November 1, and by appointment the rest of the year. Phone (703) 636-6982 or 635-2478.

Downtown Front Royal is presently getting a clean-up and restoration in order to greet its annual one million visitors more appropriately. Autumn is always the busiest time of year. Many people plan to come on the second weekend of October to celebrate the town's annual event, the Festival of Leaves. Block tickets for the quilt show, craft displays, or carriage rides can be purchased at the Chamber of Commerce. *The Bizarre Bazaar* (Chester Street; phone 636-6845) and *The Crafty Fox* (Main Street, at the courthouse; phone 825-1656) sell original handmade items and other gifts throughout the year.

A cluster of hotels and motels is located at the southern end of town in front of the entrance to the Drive. Most of them have dining rooms, but a quick drive or walk back into town offers two recommended choices. The restaurant of the *Constant Springs Inn* (413 S. Royal Avenue) has simple decor and very good meals. Phone 635-7010. *My Father's Moustache* (106 S. Royal Avenue) has everything from Maine lobster to deli sandwiches. Each dining room in this pre-Civil War home has its own theme. Phone 635-3496.

It should be noted for canoe enthusiasts that the lovely South Fork of the Shenandoah River flows past Front Royal just before it forms the main Shenandoah (see Chapter 11). There are two canoe rental companies, *Downriver Canoe Company* (10 miles south of Front Royal on U.S. 340; turn right onto SR 613 in Bentonville) and *Front Royal Canoe* (on U.S. 340, 2 miles south of Front Royal). Write: Downriver Canoe Company, Rt. 1, Box 256-A, Bentonville, VA 22610, or phone (703) 635-5526; or write: Front Royal Canoe, Rt. 1, Box 550, Front Royal, VA 22630, or phone (703) 635-5440.

Resources

Front Royal/Warren Co. Chamber of Commerce
501 S. Royal Ave.
P.O. Box 568
Front Royal, VA 22630
Tel. (703) 635-3185

10

Skyline Drive

The Skyline Drive in the Shenandoah National Park is one of America's most popular scenic highways. Its natural beauty can be appreciated at any season or time of day, but the changing colors of the leaves make fall the most spectacular season to take in the Drive. It is also the perfect time to be outdoors, as the days are still sunny but the air feels crisp. In winter it has its own special look, when the gray, foggy days blend with the blues and greens of the pine trees. Icicles hanging from rocks and waterfalls have a stunning effect when they are seen against a background of new snow. Wildflowers are the signal of warmer months to come. Then deer and other animals venture to the road and plenty of shade covers the picnic tables.

In 1934, the Shenandoah National Park was created by Congress in an attempt to preserve the mountain lands and to establish jobs by the building of roads and trails. When the Park Service personnel arrived to begin clearing, they found several mountain communities. It was not known what prompted these people to settle in the Blue Ridge, but when British and Hessian uniform buttons were found stuffed in the cracks of their log homes, it was theorized that the first inhabitants were deserters from the Revolutionary War.

Shenandoah Valley and Skyline Drive

Since colonial times the settlers had made a living through ingenious adaptations of the rocky slopes for farming and through the bartering of goods. Money was later earned by selling chestnuts or making moonshine. Each "holler" was its own neighborhood and took part in apple butter boilings and other group projects. One resident related, "You had to stay up all night for you couldn't stop once you started it boilin'. We drank moonshine, played music, and couples took turns stirrin' the apple butter. Those whar great parties!" There were also countless fights and feuds between families, reminiscent of the Hatfields and McCoys. Encounters with the "revenoors" provided lively contact with the outside world. These families were forced to leave their homes in order to make way for the Park.

Although the mountain culture no longer exists in this part of the Blue Ridge, the Park Service has preserved the history of the early settlers. Two visitor centers (at Dickey Ridge, mile 4.6, and Big Meadows, mile 51) distribute information through interpretive exhibits. Books, maps, slides, and other materials are sold. Notices of naturalist programs such as campfire talks and hikes are posted on the fifty-one bulletin boards found along the Drive. Events are also described in the Park newspaper, *Shenandoah Overlook*.

Also dotting the Drive are a small number of rustic snack bars, service stations, and gift shops that are filled with souvenirs and handcrafts. For those who prefer to leave the roadway, a network of more than five hundred miles of hiking trails covers the Park. A walk can range from a five-minute leg-stretcher to the ninety-five miles of the Appalachian Trail (see below, **Selected Hikes**).

The lodges at Skyland and Big Meadows provide overnight accommodations and meals for those who want to enjoy the countryside without sleeping in a tent. Skyland has horseback trips while Big Meadows offers wagon rides. A combination of comfort and camping can be found at Lewis Mountain Lodge.

Tunnel along Skyline Drive, Shenandoah National Park

Furnished cottages with bathrooms, lights, and heat are attached to outdoor cooking areas with picnic tables, fireplaces, and concrete floors. Reservations for all lodges should be made well in advance, particularly for the peak fall season of October 10 to 25. For information and lodge reservations write: ARA— Virginia Sky-Line Co., Inc., P.O. Box 727, Luray, VA 22835, or phone (703) 743-5108. To contact Skyland Lodge phone (703) 999-2211; to contact Big Meadows Lodge phone (703) 999-2221; to contact Lewis Mountain Lodge phone (703) 999-2255, in winter months 743-5108.

The Potomac Appalachian Trail Club (PATC) also maintains overnight accommodations. Six trail cabins can be rented and the entire length of the Appalachian Trail (AT) is accessible to backpackers. The AT is easily reached as it frequently crosses the Drive. For cabin reservations write: Potomac Appalachian Trail Club Headquarters, 1718 N St., N.W., Washington, D.C. 20036, or phone (202) 638-5306.

The Drive can also be used as a means of travel for motorists who prefer to take "the scenic route" to their destinations. There are numerous picnic areas and overlooks, many of which have markers telling about the view or past use of the land. There are, however, only four entrances to the Drive (see map), all of which charge a small admission fee. Also, with a speed limit of 35 m.p.h. and sometimes heavy traffic during peak vacation periods, it is certainly not a fast means of travel.

Selected Hikes

CAUTION: Check at the entrance station, with a ranger, or with a current map before setting out. Rerouting of the trails does occur.

#1—Between mileposts 31 and 32. From the parking lot of Panorama Visitor Center follow the Appalachian Trail south for 1.86 miles to Mary's Rock. There are spectacular views of the Valley from the rock.

#2—Between mileposts 98 and 99. From Beegle's Gap follow the Appalachian Trail approximately ½ mile. On the left is a well-worn path leading to the summit of Calf Mountain. This is a cleared summit offering a 360-degree view.

#3—Between mileposts 24 and 25. The Appalachian Trail is ¼ mile from the parking area at the west end of Elk Wallow Picnic Grounds. Follow the blue-blazed trail, which passes Jeremy's Run, one of the prettiest streams in the Park. The trail ends at the junction of two dirt roads after 6.52 miles. A circuit hike is possible by following Knob Mountain Trail, which enters from the right and returns to the picnic area (it is a steep climb to the summit of Knob Mountain).

#4—Between mileposts 39 and 40. From Skyland Visitor Center follow the marked trail 1.3 miles to the cliffs of Little Stoney Man. A circuit trip can be made by descending .21 miles to the Appalachian Trail. Turn left and follow the Appalachian Trail 1.32 miles back to Skyland.

#5—Between mileposts 42 and 43. Begin the White Oak Canyon Trail at the parking area. It is considered by many to be the Park's most picturesque hike. The last set of waterfalls is approximately 3.7 miles from the starting point.

#6—Between mileposts 81 and 82. From the Falls Trail parking area follow the blue-blazed trail to Doyle's River Cabin, where the trail joins the Appalachian Trail. Follow the Appalachian Trail left, returning to the parking area (approximately 8-mile hike). The trip can be shortened by following Browns Gap Road left before reaching the Doyle's River Cabin, completing the circuit back to the car. A 2.7-mile round trip takes hikers to the upper falls only.

#7—Sidetrip to Old Ragg Mountain. This is a massive rock peak in the northern Blue Ridge. From the beginning of the blue-blazed Nicholson Hollow Trail (1 mile from Nethers) ascend Ridge Trail to the top, descend Saddle Trail, and return to Nethers via Weakley Hollow Fire Road (approximately 7 miles).

To reach Nethers: From U.S. 29 follow business route into Madison, Va. Follow VA 231 north from Madison, take left on SR 602 to Nethers, and continue on SR 600 to beginning of trail. From Skyline Drive take Panorama Visitor Center exit on U.S. 211 to Sperryville, then follow SR 522 south for .8 mile, turn right onto SR 602 to Nethers.

The brochure which the National Park Service distributes also includes a listing of trails and overlooks. The most complete descriptions are found in *Circuit Hikes in the Shenandoah National Park* or the *Guide to the Appalachian Trail and Side Trails in the Shenandoah National Park*. Both are published by the Potomac Appalachian Trail Club (see above).

Resources

For books, maps, and slides pertaining to the park:
Shenandoah Natural History Association
Luray, VA 22835

Superintendent, Shenandoah National Park
Luray, VA 22835
(703) 999-2243

To report emergencies call (703) 999-2227
For information only call (703) 999-2266
For campground reservations call (703) 999-2282

Luray Caverns

11

Luray
and Page County

Page County lies centered in the Massanutten Valley, a lush, forested territory between the Blue Ridge and Massanutten ranges. Formed in 1831, its namesake was John Page, a member of the first U.S. Congress. Here at an Indian village on the Shenandoah River, the members of William Penn's colony located the first settlement west of the Blue Ridge.

In the early days, before any designated towns were established in this small valley, voyagers from the east were forced to travel thirty to forty miles on foot or horseback before reaching Woodstock, the closest county seat. For this reason petitions were collected and Luray was officially established. Discussion is still lively regarding the origin of the name: Luray, France; Lou Ray, the nickname of Lewis Ramsey, a town blacksmith; or the Iroquois word describing the locale are some of the possibilities.

Although no battles of major importance were fought in the county, the Civil War took its toll on the residents. When Sheridan charged his troops to turn the Valley into a site where "crows flying over will have to carry provisions," over 300 barns were burned. The farmers and their families were devastated.

Prior to 1881, wagons and flatbottom boats hauled goods in and out of the area along the Shenandoah River. When the Manassas Gap Railroad connected with Woodstock, the nature of transportation in the Valley was forever changed. In 1881, the railroad added Luray to its network, sparking the greatest economic boom in the county's history.

Points of Interest

Luray Caverns (follow U.S. 211 to Luray and follow the signs; entrance is just beyond western city limits) are Page County's main attraction. These formations are the largest of their type in the Eastern United States, drawing nearly half a million visitors annually. A stalactite organ, rocks that look like fried eggs, and a natural wishing well are some of the spectacles pointed out during a tour. Open daily 9 to 5 winter, 9 to 6 spring and fall, 9 to 7 summer. Closed Christmas Day. Admission charge. Write: Luray Caverns, Box 748, Luray, VA 22835, or phone (703) 743-6551. Nearby is the *Luray singing tower* (next to entrance to caverns), a forty-seven-bell carillon featured in regular recitals. Concerts at 2 P.M. and 8 P.M. daily, in spring only. Free. Also close by is a reptile center (on U.S. 211, ½ mile from caverns). Restaurant chains and motels are located close to these sites.

The several blocks of downtown Luray are filled with shops, businesses, and several pleasant cafes and restaurants. *The Brookside Restaurant* (4 miles north of Luray on U.S. 211) is where many residents go for family dining and superb home cooking. Picnics to go can be ordered. Phone (703) 743-5698. *The Parkhurst Restaurant* (4 miles south of Luray on U.S. 211) caters to evening diners by serving international cuisine. Phone (703) 743-6009.

In Page County there is a spectacular stretch of the South Fork Shenandoah River. In *Virginia White Water* (Springfield, Virginia: 1977) H. Roger Corbett writes, "The South Fork

Shenandoah is, without a doubt, a river without parallel in the United States. . . . To attempt a description of its 102.5 miles in a single volume is almost an affront to such a beautiful and magnificent stream." Some of the river can be seen by following SR 684. *Shenandoah River Outfitters* (at traffic lights in Luray turn north on U.S. 340 for 1 block; turn left onto Mechanic St.; go 4 miles; turn right onto SR 684 for 6 miles) rents canoes, camping gear, and inner tubes and will also plan guided day or overnight trips. Phone (703) 743-4159.

Resources

Page County Chamber of Commerce
Main Street
Luray, VA 22835
Tel. (703) 743-3915

View from the Blue Ridge Parkway

12

Harrisonburg
and Rockingham County

Hoping to find religious freedom, Adam Miller left Germany with his wife and sister to become Rockingham County's first settlers in 1726. In their small log cabin, the family survived Indian attacks and a great fire. They began selling parcels of land to other Germans eager to begin a new life. In 1777 the county was established and named for Charles Watson Wentworth Rockingham, a British prime minister sympathetic toward the colonists. Two years later, Thomas Harrison laid out fifty acres of his land and sold them in lots to create the town of Harrisonburg, which became the county seat.

Abraham Lincoln's great-grandfather, known as "Virginia John," was an early resident of the county. His son, the president's grandfather, was a Virginia captain during the Revolutionary War. After independence was won, the Lincolns moved to Kentucky, leaving the Virginia homestead to Great-Uncle Jacob.

The Civil War also brought a Rockingham County resident into national prominence. As Stonewall Jackson's cavalry leader, General Turner Ashby was invaluable as a spy and a soldier. Despite his high military rank, Ashby refused to give up his place on the battlefield beside his men. He was killed in fighting on the outskirts of Harrisonburg.

Few might recognize the name of Samuel Blosser, but he too made a lasting impact on the county's history. In 1884 he put chicken eggs in a box of sawdust and kept them warm by the kitchen stove. When the chicks hatched three weeks later, the poultry industry was on its way. Many Thanksgiving dinners now originate in Rockingham, "Turkey Capital of the World."

Points of Interest

With James Madison University situated close to the town center, Harrisonburg is in some ways like any small college town. Along with the busy student life, however, there is a community with strong agricultural ties. In Rockingham County, the southern and eastern sections (particularly around Dayton) are pastoral. They have been influenced by the Mennonite community, and it is not uncommon to see a horse and buggy parked outside a small grocery store. The north and west are more mountainous and remote. Uniting the different districts are the many farms and factories of the poultry industry.

Places to visit begin with the *Warren-Sipe Museum* in Harrisonburg (301 S. Main Street), where an electric map recounts Stonewall Jackson's phenomenal campaign. His unorthodox strategy was invented by necessity when his 17,000 troops were matched against 60,000 Union soldiers. Open 10 to 4 Tuesday to Saturday, April 1 to December 15. Admission charge. Phone (703) 434-4762. In nearby Dayton is the *Daniel Harrison House* (on SR 42 business in Dayton), a restored home which was once used as a fort during Indian attacks. Open 1 to 5 Friday to Sunday, April 27 to October 14. Closed at other times except by appointment. Free. Phone (703) 879-2280. Also found in the county are *Massanutten*

Caverns (from Harrisonburg take U.S. 33 east to Keezletown; turn left onto SR 620; go 2½ miles; turn right onto SR 685 to caverns) and *Grand Caverns* (take exit 60 from I-81, between Staunton and Harrisonburg, then go east for 6 miles). Both are open to the public with guided tours. Grand Caverns, now a regional park, was once used by Jackson to quarter his troops and horses and later became a setting for fancy balls and elaborate, postbellum entertainment. Admission charge. For information about Massanutten Caverns phone (703) 269-6555, about Grand Caverns phone (703) 249-5705 (if no answer phone 249-5729).

The opportunities for finding something fun to do extend beyond the registered historical landmarks. Downtown Harrisonburg has a number of second-hand and antique stores mixed in with the shops around the downtown Court Square. Also James Madison University (on U.S. 11) intermittently schedules plays, concerts, and other presentations. For general information phone (703) 568-6211; for theatre box office phone (703) 568-6260. The best way to get a sense of rural living is to attend the *Rockingham County Fair.* Tractor pulls, livestock shows, and a baby beauty contest are all part of the scheduled events, making this one of the best county fairs in the Valley. Admission charge. For information write: Rockingham County Fair Association, P.O. Box 501, Harrisonburg, VA 22801 or phone (703) 434-0005.

In the middle of the county, *Massanutten Mountain* rises up abruptly from level farmlands. The mountain is a part of the George Washington National Forest and spreads into the neighboring counties of Shenandoah, Page, and Warren. Information on the picnic sites and hiking trails, which are well marked and easily accessible, can be found at the visitor center (on U.S. 211 between New Market and Luray). Phone (703) 740-8310. A special Braille trail enhances the forest experience for the blind. Also found on the mountain are the remains of the *Catherine Furnace* and *Elizabeth Furnace* (on SR

678, approximately 10 miles south of Strasburg), where iron was once produced. Another interesting site for picnickers is Camp Roosevelt, where the first Civilian Conservation Corps Camp was built during the Depression years of the 1930s. The variety of places to eat is in keeping with the nature of the territory. *Jess's Quick Lunch* in Harrisonburg (22 S. Main) is an immensely popular hot dog diner. When it burned down several years ago, its rebuilding was a community effort. Phone (703) 434-8282. Also in the neighborhood is *Spanky's* (60 W. Water Street) a delicatessen that the "Our Gang" generation wouldn't want to miss. Phone (703) 434-7647. The *Ole Virginia Ham Cafe* (85 West Market Street) is a good spot for breakfast. Phone (703) 434-2626.

For assistance in finding overnight accommodations, the Shenandoah Valley Bed and Breakfast Reservations has a listing of available hosts who offer this service. Write: Shenandoah Valley Bed and Breakfast Reservations, P.O. Box 305, Broadway, VA 22815, or phone (703) 896-9702 or 896-2579 4 P.M. to 11 P.M.

Resources

George Washington National Forest—Forest Service
210 Federal Bldg.
Harrisonburg, VA 22801
(703) 433-2491

Harrisonburg–Rockingham Chamber of Commerce
191 South Main St., P.O. Box 1
Harrisonburg, VA 22801
(703) 434-3862

13

Staunton
and Augusta County

A location in the scenic heartland and a rich history contribute to the distinctive personality of the Staunton-Augusta area. The Queen City of the Shenandoah Valley and the surrounding county were a starting point for many westward journeys of pioneer days. Owing to its central Virginia location, many state and private institutions were established here. As a result, the area benefitted culturally, educationally, and economically.

Descendants of the early settlers and newer residents have joined together to create a strong family community. One town project has been a revitalization of the downtown area. Over forty businesses and the Wharf warehouse district have received facelifts and restorations. A recent development is the building of the Museum of American Frontier Culture. Authentic farmsteads from seventeenth and eighteenth century England, Northern Ireland, and Germany will be reconstructed just outside Staunton.

The charm of the Staunton area lies in her beautiful old homes, her history as a crossroads for early travelers, and her unique position between her rural neighbors spreading to West Virginia and the more contemporary Virginia to the east.

Staunton and Augusta County

History

The story of Staunton and Augusta County begins in Ireland, where a daring young Scotch-Irish man named John Lewis refused to pay his rent after it was unfairly raised. Late one night, the owner of the property, Lord Clonmithgarin, came to the Lewis castle with armed followers, and in the ensuing battle the lord was slain. John Lewis feared that his act of self-defense would be interpreted as murder. With his wife, Margaret, he fled to the Valley of Virginia. He embarked on a new life in a traditional log cabin which was called "Bellefont." Soon Lewis and other Scotch-Irish pioneers surrounded their settlement with a stockade and blockhouses to protect them from the Indians. Margaret Lewis proudly noted in her diary, "It shall descend to his posterity that John Lewis hath builded the first town in the Valley."

Four years after Lewis's arrival, the governor of Virginia, William Gooch, granted 118,491 acres of land to William Beverley, a close friend and member of the Governor's Council. In the area which is now Augusta County, Beverley constructed a mill; it acquired the name of Beverley's Mill Place.

In 1738, the General Assembly of the Colony of Virginia declared that the land on either side of the Blue Ridge would be separated. The western section was named Augusta County in honor of the wife of King George II. Just one year later, Beverley set aside twenty-five acres to be used as a town. It was named after Lady Rebecca Staunton, wife of Governor Gooch.

During the Revolutionary War, Staunton served as a meeting place for the Colonial Assembly. Our nation's leaders, including Thomas Jefferson and Patrick Henry, were hiding in Trinity Church following their pursuit by the British General Tarleton. Legend says that as word reached the Assemblymen that Tarleton was on his way to Staunton, Patrick Henry lost his boot in the churchyard while making a

Birthplace of Woodrow Wilson, 28th President of the United States, in Staunton

hasty escape. He and his fleeing comrades were forced to spread out in different directions under the night sky.

Staunton and Augusta County prospered during the post-Revolutionary War years as a prime location for travelers to begin their westward journeys. Institutions such as Mary Baldwin College and the Virginia School for the Deaf and Blind were founded. By the time of the Civil War, this central Valley location was chosen as a supply depot and temporary headquarters for Gen. Stonewall Jackson. Despite General Sheridan's devastation of the Valley, Staunton continued to attract residents.

In the years to come and in the shadow of both World Wars, many industries were started, transferring the base of the economy from a strictly agrarian one to one combining industry and agriculture. The junction of two major interstate highways at the edge of town draws visitors and businesses and upholds the tradition that Staunton is at a crossroads.

Places to Visit/Things to Do

McCormick's Farm (25 miles southeast of Staunton on U.S. 11 and I-81). Step back 150 years to the time when Cyrus McCormick invented the first successful reaper. Visitors can tour the authentic mill and workshop. Open Monday to Friday, evenings and on weekends by appointment. Free. Picnic area. Phone (703) 377-2255.

Natural Chimneys (7 miles southwest of Bridgewater on SR 731, in Mt. Solon). The Natural Chimneys were carved from limestone as the sea that once covered the area receded. The stone towers rise up 120 feet above the rolling valley floor and provide the scenery for an annual jousting tournament (see under **Seasonal Events**). Admission charge. Phone 350-2510.

Statler Brothers Museum (501 Thornrose Avenue). Country music fans will enjoy the mini-museum of Staunton's famous music group. Tours offered at 2 P.M. Monday to Friday. Gift shop open 10:30 to 3:30 Monday to Friday. Free.

Staunton Braves Baseball Games. Pick up some peanuts and cheer on a 125-year-old, semi-professional team at the John Moxie Memorial Stadium (adjacent to Gypsy Hill Park). Call the Staunton Chamber of Commerce for game times 886-2351.

Staunton Fine Arts Association (at the entrance of Gypsy Hill Park on Churchill Ave.). Each month a regional artist is selected to exhibit current works at the gallery. The Association frequently hosts receptions at which visitors can meet the artist. Free. Phone 885-2028.

Walking Tour of Staunton. Walking through the streets of Staunton is the best way to appreciate the many fine design features of the old homes and businesses. Free tour brochures are available at the Travel Information Center, Chamber of Commerce, Woodrow Wilson Birthplace, and area hotels and motels.

The gardens at Woodrow Wilson's birthplace in Staunton

Woodrow Wilson Birthplace (24 N. Coalter Street). Tour the Greek revival town house where our twenty-eighth president was born. Special attractions include President Wilson's childhood furniture, his Pierce-Arrow White House limousine, and a Victorian garden. Open 9 to 5 daily except Christmas, New Years, and Thanksgiving, and Sundays in December, January, and February. Closing time extended to 6 P.M. in summer months. Admission charge. Phone 885-0897.

Mary Baldwin College (Frederick Street). The college supports lectures, theatre productions, musical events, and art shows, which are open to the public. Admission charge to some events. For information phone 887-7000; for theatre phone 887-7188.

Apple and Peach Picking. Virginia is especially famous for its apples. Many orchards invite visitors to pick their own or stop by roadside stands for fresh fruit and cider. Check the local paper for orchard locations and hours.

Oak Grove Theatre. Summer skies and Valley woodlands are the scenery for talented local actors performing the annual series of plays. Contact the Chamber of Commerce for ticket information and directions to the theatre's Verona location.

Shopping

The primary shopping areas in downtown Staunton are The Wharf and Main Street. The Wharf district begins at *The Factory* (112 South New Street) of the renovated White Star Mills. Found here is *Of Things Past* (112-B S. New Street), an antique shop where a couple of steps will take you from early America to the Orient through the Art Deco period of the 30s. The owner (who happens to be the mother of one of the authors) always has a cup of tea ready for anyone who has time to browse or chat. Phone 885-6040. Following the train tracks down Middlebrook Avenue, one finds the studios of painters and craftsmen, who periodically display their work. More antique shops and gift boutiques are to be found in this area.

Walking up to Beverley Street, one finds *Turtle Lane* (10 E. Beverley Street), which always has a show window that draws customers inside. The shop's antiques, gifts, and fanciful toys create a combination shop and gallery. Phone 886-9313. On Frederick Street is the *Woodrow Wilson Birthplace Gift Shop* (230 E. Frederick Street), a small house that keeps its rooms arranged with fine pewter, table settings, and decorative kitchen tools. Phone 885-3461.

Dining

The Beverley Restaurant (12 E. Beverley Street). This favorite watering hole could serve as a scene for a Norman Rockwell painting. The restaurant's slogan says: "Everything is made fresh every day. When it's gone it's gone." Don't leave

Staunton without a piece of the Beverley Restaurant's wonderful pie. Phone 886-4317.

The Buckhorn Inn (13 miles west of Staunton on U.S. 250). This early nineteenth century tavern's homecooked meals are served family style, along with a country buffet. The Buckhorn has a resident "ghost," a forest setting, and tables by the fireside. (See also **Lodging**.) Phone 337-6900.

Edelweiss Restaurant (take exit 55 on I-81). Similarities between the Black Forest and Blue Ridge Mountains drew the Rosler family to Augusta County. They prepare traditional German specialties daily for their Old World restaurant. Phone 337-1203.

McCormick's Pub and Restaurant (41 N. Augusta Street). This elegant dining room was once an old Y.M.C.A. building. The original clerical desk has been transformed into a curved bar, and the tile floors and black walnut woodwork have been refinished. Distinctive entrees such as roast duck in port wine sauce are available from a large menu. A pub selection is also offered for a lighter meal. Bakery is open to the public at 8 A.M. Phone 885-3111.

Wharf Deli and Pub (123 Augusta Street). Thick sandwiches and daily specials are served in an attractive, airy environment. It is easy to splurge on imported wine and beer and a sinful pastry. Phone 886-2329.

White Star Mills (Mill Street, across from The Factory shops). Stained-glass windows filter light into this restored flour mill. An extensive, well-prepared menu is offered in surroundings which recall Staunton's early days. Many people from around the county travel here to celebrate their special occasions. Phone 885-3409.

Lodging

Belle Grae Inn (515 Frederick Street). Guests at this restored Victorian mansion can walk to the historic downtown area. Tea or sherry is served on the shaded porch or in front of one of the seven fireplaces. Phone 886-5151.

Buckhorn Inn (13 miles west of Staunton on U.S. 250). A winding staircase and a graceful Southern façade have been restored in this country tavern. Once a place where the sick and wounded were nursed during the Civil War, the building went through many hands before the present owners reestablished it as an inn. The interior is furnished with antiques, and the wide veranda and wicker rockers entice guests to linger and enjoy the cool mountain air. Phone 885-2900.

Frederick House (Frederick and New streets). Three town houses built between 1810 and 1910 have been combined to make an attractive inn with room for forty-three guests. Across the street from Mary Baldwin College, it is in the heart of the downtown historic district. Phone 885-4220.

Recreation

Betsy Bell City Park (Greenville Avenue). Driving into Staunton from U.S. 250 East, visitors see two small mountains to their left called Betsy Bell and Mary Gray. One mountain bears the shape of a cross cut into the foliage. A fifty-acre nature park exists here with trails and campsites.

The names of the mountains date back to the time when the early settler John Lewis and his neighbors would retell one of their favorite legends from their home in Ireland. Two young girls named Betsy Bell and Mary Gray were known throughout Scotland for their beauty and devoted friendship. When the plague broke out, their fathers safeguarded them deep in the forest. However, one of the girls discovered a way to continue meeting with her lover, while the other girl remained a true friend by keeping the secret. Both girls contracted the plague and died.

George Washington National Forest. Stretching across the western boundaries of Augusta County, the George

Washington National Forest is an ideal recreation site. Fishermen can try their luck in secluded streams or bring their families to one of the recreation areas at Todd Lake (follow SR 730 west from Natural Chimneys Regional Park for approximately 7 miles), North River (stay on SR 730 west past Todd Lake and watch for sign), or Braley Pond (follow U.S. 250 W, turn right onto SR 715). Hikers in search of a spectacular panorama can climb *Elliot's Knob* (follow U.S. 250 W approximately 17 miles from Staunton, turn left onto SR 629; it is between Shenandoah Mountain and North Mountain), the highest peak in the Forest.

Ramsey's Draft Wilderness Area (on U.S. 250 W between North Mountain and Shenandoah Mountain). No pioneers ever settled the steep and rocky hillsides of this portion of the George Washington National Forest. Ferns, delicate wildflowers, and towering hemlocks can be seen by campers and wanderers who roam this virgin forest. A sign and picnic ground mark the main entrance.

Sherando Lake (follow SR 664 south from Waynesboro for approximately 8 miles). The George Washington National Forest surrounds the lake and recreation area. There is a nice sandy beach and a separate canoeing and fishing area. Admission charge.

Gypsy Hill Park (Churchill Avenue). When gypsies traveled through the Valley, they camped at this site on the edge of town. As the city grew it encircled the area, creating a park which remains a focal recreation and gathering place. Families of all ages pass the time feeding swans, riding the kiddie train, or coaxing the peacocks to show off their colors. Active visitors may play tennis or golf, jog, swim, or team up for a game of baseball. Seasonally, the park hosts municipal band concerts, art shows, and tennis tournaments.

Seasonal Events

Woodrow Wilson Birthplace Events (24 N. Coalter Street). On Presidents' Day the guides dress in period costumes for George Washington's birthday. A needlework show is scheduled in May and an antique show and sale is held in the garden in September. Woodrow Wilson's birthday is the occasion for an open house on December 28. Admission charge. Phone 885-0897.

Staunton Fine Arts Association Arts and Crafts Festival. Amidst old trees and graceful swans in Gypsy Hill Park (Churchville Avenue), area artists exhibit their work at a juried show. May. Free.

Natural Chimneys Jousting Tournament (Mt. Solon). Medieval games unfold against the background of natural stone turrets. Since 1821, Natural Chimneys has been the site for annual tournaments in the ancient art of jousting, making this the oldest continuous sporting event in the country. Third Saturday in August. Hall of Fame Competition held in June. Admission charge. Phone 350-2510.

Happy Birthday U.S.A. Staunton's native sons, the Statler Brothers, invite a featured recording star to join them in a down home Fourth of July celebration. Their concert highlights a weekend filled with local country and bluegrass bands, a vesper service, and gospel singers. Bring your own folding chairs and blankets to spread out among tens of thousands of onlookers at a unique Independence Day weekend. Most events free. For information write: P.O. Box 266, Staunton, VA 24401, or phone (703) 886-3714.

Stonewall Jackson Brigade Band Concerts. The well-loved 126-year-old municipal band continues its tradition every summertime Monday night in the gazebo at Gypsy Hill Park. Free.

Mennonite Relief Sale and Quilt Auction (held at Augusta Expoland in Fishersville). Huge black cauldrons of apple butter and Brunswick stew simmer while waiting to be ladled out atop thick slices of homemade bread. Intricate quilts are auctioned off, and crafts, baked goods, and furniture are also for sale. Early October. Free. For information write: Mennonite Relief Sale and Quilt Auction, Box 608, Waynesboro, VA 22980 or phone 943-8987.

Resources

Augusta County Historical Society.
Local historians have researched and published Valley history. Their journals and other works can be found at the Staunton Public Library (Market Street). Consult the Chamber of Commerce for the phone number of a contact person.

Historic Staunton Foundation
P.O. Box 2534
Staunton, Virginia 24401
(703) 885-7676

Staunton-Augusta County Chamber of Commerce
P.O. Box 389
Staunton, Virginia 24401
(703) 886-2351

Travel Information Center
U.S. 250 East at the junction of I-64 and I-81
(703) 885-8504

14

Waynesboro

Waynesboro was originally included in the large parcel of land granted to William Beverley by King George II. After three years William Tees acquired a sizable tract from Beverley and called it Teesville. In later years, his daughter-in-law, Mary Reid, a young widow, began to sell lots from the inherited acreage to help support her family. She was also forced to open her home as a tavern. Thomas Jefferson often stayed the night there on his journeys through the Valley.

As did most small settlements on the Western territories of the new nation, Waynesboro had its problems with the Indians. Therefore, when Gen. "Mad Anthony" Wayne, famous for his role in the War of Independence, protected the border towns against further attack, Teesville was renamed in his honor.

Waynesboro continued to develop as a community. Churches, businesses, and a school were built. The site for today's city hall formerly surrounded a spring which provided the area's drinking water. At one time, going down for a drink at the spring was a social occasion, offering a chance to catch up on Waynesboro news and gossip.

Although several places were shelled at times, Waynesboro received few battle scars during the Civil War. The town physician, Dr. Fulton, impartially treated the wounded from both sides. He slipped Confederate patients through a hole in the wall to hiding whenever the Union Army marched through.

By 1889, nearby Basic City had become a small factory community. Thirty-five years later it merged with Waynesboro and became an industrial center for the Shenandoah Valley.

The highest concentration of industry today is still at the old Basic City site, although other small factories and plants have grown up alongside the small farming communities on the outskirts of town. Waynesboro still supports an active and vital downtown district. Most businesses and shopping are located on or near Main Street.

Points of Interest

One of the first places that sightseers stop is the *Virginia Metalcrafters Showroom and Factory* (at eastern entrance to Waynesboro, on U.S. 250). A windowed balcony permits visitors, before they do their shopping, to watch the brass items being produced. An annual sale is held the weekend after Thanksgiving. Phone 949-8205.

Another well-known stop-off is the *Purple Foot* (1035 W. Main Street), which began as a small gourmet shop and grew into a busy cafe. Whether the customer is having a long lunch or a cup of exotic tea, there is no rushed feeling at this restaurant. A fountain, big umbrellas, and flowers decorate the outdoor patio, which is open during pleasant weather. The fare consists of sandwiches, quiches, salads, and homemade soup. (Lunch only.) Phone 949-9463.

Waynesboro's major event is the *Fall Foliage Festival*. Coolness in the air heightens the excitement of week-long fundraisers and roadraces. Main Street is closed off for a regional art show and local clubs fix specialties to make sure that no one goes hungry. October. For information write Waynesboro Chamber of Commerce.

At nearby *Stuarts Draft* (follow U.S. 340 west) the continuous fences and pastures that give the Valley its character reappear. Stuarts Draft is known for its Mom and Pop businesses and immaculate Mennonite farms. Located at one of these farms is the *Kinzinger Kountry Kitchen* (SR 142 and SR 190), where the shelves are piled with freshly baked breads, rolls, and cakes. Phone 337-2668. Down the lane is the *Cheese Shop* (SR 608, 1 mile north of Stuarts Draft's only traffic light), another Mennonite business where cheeses, bulk grains, dried fruits, and nuts may be bought at bargain prices. Phone 337-4224.

Also in the area is the *Candy Shop* (U.S. 340 North), which gives customers the chance to sample the products of the nearby Hershey Chocolate Factory. Originally a 1923 schoolhouse, the Candy Shop now supports several stores, offices, and a restaurant. Phone 337-1438.

Resources

Waynesboro–East Augusta Chamber of Commerce
P.O. Box 459
Waynesboro, VA 22980
(703) 949-8203

Blue Ridge Parkway

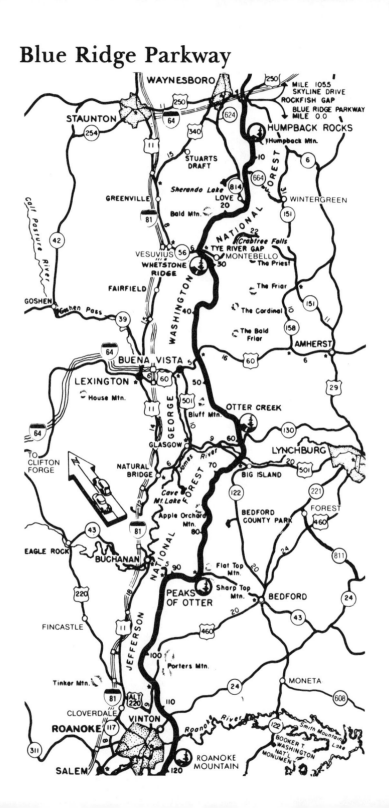

15

Blue Ridge Parkway

The symbol of the white pine guides motorists down the Blue Ridge Parkway, a scenic highway which overlooks wide vistas of Shenandoah Valley territory. Created in 1936, the Parkway's purpose was to connect Virginia's Shenandoah National Park with the Great Smoky Mountains National Park in Tennessee and North Carolina. The entire stretch covers 470 miles, with only one section still under construction in North Carolina.

The Parkway begins at the Afton Mountain interchange of Interstate 64 between Charlottesville and Waynesboro. No tolls or fees are charged. *Swannanoa,* an Italian Renaissance palace, is located near the entrance and is open for tours. Two philosophers, Lao and Walter Russell, restored the estate many years ago and established their "University of Science and Philosophy." Today the ornate marble interior, murals, and a Tiffany stained-glass window hint at an earlier splendor. Admission charge.

Easy-to-follow mileposts which begin at 0 at the Afton entrance mark the Parkway. At milepost 5 is the first visitor center, where a pioneer homestead appears. The many ingenious methods of farming and providing shelter have been recreated and described on a self-guided walk. Across the road lies Humpback Rocks, where a steep hike is rewarded with views of hazy blue mountains and miniature farms.

Continuing down the Parkway one finds more small visitor centers, self-guided trails, and overlooks. Ravens Roost (milepost 10.7) is a good picnic spot where both hang gliders and rock climbers take advantage of the elevated cliffs. The *Peaks of Otter* at milepost 84 is a friendly mountain lodge with overnight accommodations for those who wish to extend their stay in the middle of the Blue Ridge. Simple pondside rooms, with no television or phones, make a night here a true getaway. The lodge has a tavern and a fine dining room which often serves local specialties. For information write: Peaks of Otter Lodge, Box 489, Bedford, VA 24523, or phone (703) 586-1081.

As the Parkway passes through Nelson County it intersects with SR 664 (Reeds Gap exit) to bring travelers to *Wintergreen,* a resort known for its skiing, dining, and gallery of shops. This vacation community adds a little luxury to the mountains' more rustic pleasures. For information call Wintergreen, Inc. at 800-325-2200. At the intersection of VA 56 (milepost 27), a trip down the hillside will lead to Crabtree Falls, a recreational area in the George Washington National Forest. Named for its bank of thundering water, it is a popular place for picnics and day hikes. Free.

Fall is the peak period for tourism. Virginians and many visitors from out of state who are not fortunate enough to have a brilliant autumn close to home take this drive as an annual rite. In colder months, when stormy weather makes driving dangerous, the road is closed. At this time the Parkway becomes a long, snow-covered avenue perfect for cross-country skiing and hiking. In mild weather, spring wildflowers, bird watching, and summer lazing draw both visitors and locals. Driving at night provides the opportunity to see the more reclusive wildlife.

The Parkway has become a welcome option to those who

have time to skip the interstate in exchange for a drive through the treetops.

Resources

Blue Ridge Parkway Association
P.O. Box 475
Asheville, NC 28802

Home of General Thomas J. "Stonewall" Jackson in Lexington

16

Lexington
and Rockbridge County

Rockbridge County enjoys a view of the Blue Ridge and Allegheny Mountains as they draw close together. Just below the city the Shenandoah Valley ends geographically.

Historic Lexington serves as the region's business and retail center. Cobblestone sidewalks, traditional college campuses, and restored brick homes and offices make up the downtown area. The final resting places for two Civil War heroes, Gen. Stonewall Jackson and Gen. Robert E. Lee, are close by.

It would seem that on almost every street something of note took place. An excellent visitor center and detailed walking tours ensure that Lexington's famous and interesting spots will not be missed. One bronze plaque hints that although obviously proud of their prestigious past, the residents are not too stuffy. The monument reads "N.O.N." indicating that nothing of historical value happened there.

History

As was true for many busy Valley towns, Lexington grew up close to a major travel route, the West Trail (now U.S. 60). As pioneers moved westward, many began their journey to the wilderness on Old Plank Road, where wood was laid to keep wagons out of the mud.

The Scotch-Irish were the primary settlers of the local communities. Having fled their native lands because of religious persecution, they were extremely strong in their Presbyterian faith. Families attended sermons several times a week and on most of Sunday. This accounts for the surprising number of old churches found throughout Rockbridge County. Many continue to hold Sunday services.

In 1896, a huge fire caught and blazed beyond control throughout Lexington. Since most of the buildings were built of logs, the town was razed. After experiencing the hazards of building with wood, residents reconstructed their homes and businesses in handsome red brick; these buildings still stand as modern Lexington's historic center.

When Liberty Hall Academy opened in 1749, Lexington's tradition as an educational center began. George Washington became a major benefactor, and the school was renamed Washington College in his honor. After the Civil War, the board of trustees asked Robert E. Lee to assume its presidency. Lee, anxious to counter the ill effects of the war and work toward something positive, accepted the position. Here he was reacquainted with many men who had fought with him against the North. He worked diligently and firmly established the school as a fine institution. Upon his death it became known as Washington and Lee University.

Lexington's other major school, Virginia Military Institute, took its beginnings from the locally stationed arsenal. It quickly expanded and proudly employed Stonewall Jackson as an instructor up until the time of the Civil War. The V.M.I. cadets took an active role in this war at the Battle of New Market. As a result, many of the school's buildings were destroyed by Federal order.

Around the turn of the century, real estate fever hit the

county. Land developers envisioned the rural towns of Buena Vista, Goshen, and Glasgow as Valley resorts. The only hotel building which remains from these unrealized plans is now the Main Hall of Southern Seminary Junior College.

The entrance of the railroad further defined the emerging pattern of the area's economic bases. Developing industry and commerce in small communities was strengthened, while the rural sections relied on farming and agriculture.

The description of farms and communities as small and closely knit still holds true of the county today. In the city, thousands of visitors arrive annually to see the colleges and historic buildings. Nevertheless, it has not become a "tourist town." The excellent visitor programs accommodate large numbers of the guests into the daily routines of the townfolk. Thus the original flavor of the area has been preserved.

Places to Visit/Things to Do

Natural Bridge (U.S. 11 south of Lexington, follow signs). Here stands one of the seven natural wonders of the world. Indian tribes used the bridge as a passageway and fortress and it was worshipped by them as "The Bridge of God." As the Valley became settled, Lord Fairfax commissioned George Washington to survey the bridge. As he completed his work he carved his initials into the stone face, and they can still be seen today. Thomas Jefferson became the first American owner when he paid twenty shillings for the property.

This impressive stone arch stands 215 feet high, 90 feet long and 150 feet wide. It holds up a U.S. highway and connects two mountains. A pageant and light show, the *Drama of Creation,* begins each evening at dark. Close by, children can enjoy the petting zoo, wax museum, and underground caverns (with a resident ghost).

Bridge open 7 A.M. to dusk daily, year round. Admission charge. Phone (703) 291-2121.

Cadets in dress parade at Virginia Military Institute in Lexington

Henry Street Playhouse. A variety of plays ranging from popular musicals to the classics is produced by local actors and theatre craftsmen. Presented in the Washington and Lee Theatre in the summer. For information contact the visitor center (address below).

Rockbridge Concert-Theatre Series. Local entertainment, traveling theatre, and dance and music groups are brought into town throughout the year.

Stonewall Jackson House (8 E. Washington Street). Unfortunately, Jackson never returned from the Civil War. His home, however, has been restored to the way it looked in the 1800s when he was an instructor at V.M.I. This was the only residence he ever owned and many of his personal belongings and furnishings have been collected here for display. Admission charge. Phone 463-2552.

Marshall Library (at Virginia Military Institute). This library contains the personal papers and documents of George

Marshall, creator of the Marshall Plan for the rebuilding of Europe after World War II. He was the first professional soldier to be honored as a Nobel Peace Prize recipient. The library is an active research facility open to scholars and historians. Free tours and special programs can be arranged. Free. Phone (703) 463-7103.

Washington and Lee University. As the sixth oldest college in the country, Washington and Lee dates back to a 1749 one-room log cabin opened by Robert Alexander. It was the first classical school in the Valley. George Washington and Robert E. Lee are credited with the survival and success of the school: Washington donated his shares in the James River Co. and afforded financial security, while Lee's leadership as president guided the College to a prominent academic position. On the campus grounds, Lee's office and the chapel where he is interred are open to the public. One of the nation's finest portrait collections, of the Washington-Custis-Lee families, is on permanent exhibition. Free. For information call 463-8400 (switchboard) or 463-8768 (Lee Chapel).

Virginia Military Institute. This institution is the oldest state-supported military college in the nation. Claudius Crozet, the famous surveyor, was the first president of the board. Stonewall Jackson taught philosophy and artillery tactics before he left for his Civil War duties, and Matthew Maury, "Pathfinder of the Seas," was also an instructor.

The V.M.I. Museum houses many artifacts from cadets who have attended this college. Stories of professor and soldier Jackson, Nobel laureate G. C. Marshall, and the "boy soldiers" who fought in the Civil War are told through museum displays. Free. Phone (703) 463-6201.

Stonewall Jackson Memorial Cemetery (South Main Street). Jackson and hundreds of Confederate soldiers lie buried here. The memorial statue of the general faces South—". . . the only time Jackson turned his back on the North." Free. Phone 463-2931.

Maple Hall, a historic country inn, in Lexington

Shopping

In Lexington, modern malls have no place. Stores, restaurants, and antique shops are found in historic buildings and around the corner from national landmarks. *Lexington Galleries* (16 N. Main) combines colonial furnishings with pewter pieces unique to the area. Phone 463-6008. The *Old Main Street Mall* (29 N. Old Main) building and *Stonewall Jackson House* (8 E. Washington) offer a number of small shops for browsers or buyers. For Stonewall Jackson House phone 463-2552.

Dining

Lexington has a number of interesting cafes and small restaurants. *The Palms* (101 W. Nelson) has tropical trees, ceiling fans, and pink decor which bring a light contrast to a day spent viewing the historic dwellings of early settlers and war heroes. Settle in for a full dinner, a fountain treat or drink at the bar. Phone 463-7911. *Spanky's* (110 S. Jefferson) puts together deli sandwiches and soups in memory of the "Our Gang" personalities who smile down from the walls. Phone 463-3338. The *Southern Inn* (37 S. Main) is the place for those looking for an authentic country dinner. Phone 463-3612.

Lodging

Alexander Withrow House Inn (3 West Washington Street). The original town house home of William Alexander weathered the years since 1789 as a school, a bank, and a store before its restoration as an inn. Phone (703) 463-2044.

The McCampbell Inn (11 N. Main Street). This counterpart to Alexander Withrow House Inn is also located in the center of Lexington and formerly housed many town services. Between 1809 and 1982 it has been John McCampbell's home, a jewelry store, a telegraph and post office, and a hotel. Phone (703) 463-2044.

Recreation

Chessie Nature Trail. The trail is a seven-mile nature trail along the former bed of the Chesapeake and Ohio Railroad. The walk begins at the original historic entrance into Lexington (where Woods Creek flows into Maury River, 25 feet west of U.S. 11 bridge). It continues to Buena Vista, crossing an island and passing several old homes and surviving portions of the canal and dam system. Parking and picnic site.

Central Academic Building, Washington & Lee University in Lexington

Goshen Pass (approximately 8 miles southeast of Goshen, 12 miles northwest of Lexington on VA 39). The pass has been carved by the Maury River, and the towering slopes and high hedges of rhododendron provide one of the best views in the county. Hiking, fishing, picnicking, swimming, and tubing can all be enjoyed. Shelters, tables, and toilet facilities are available at the wayside.

George Washington National Forest. An intricate system of trails and circular hikes has been developed in this area of the forest, known as the Pedlar District. Information and maps for hiking, camping, fishing, and canoeing are available from the Pedlar District Ranger's Office, 2424 Magnolia Avenue, Buena Vista, VA 24416; phone (703) 261-6105. One section includes the James River Wilderness Area.

James River Basin Canoe Livery, Ltd. Overnight river camping and fishing trips are arranged for any level of expertise. Open year round. For information write: James River Basin Canoe Livery, Ltd., RFD 4, Buena Vista, VA 24416, or phone (703) 261-7334.

Seasonal Events

Stonewall Jackson House (8 E. Washington Street). Throughout December, the general's home is decorated for Christmas in Victorian style. Caroling, craft demonstrations, and workshops are some of the special activities planned. Jackson's birthday on January 21 is celebrated with free tours and refreshments. Admission charge. Phone (703) 463-2552.

Rockbridge Community Festival. Over 170 professional and amateur craftsmen display their work at this one-day fair. Local musicians provide entertainment and civic groups sponsor shows for children. August. Free. For information write: P.O. Box 1095, Lexington, VA 22456.

Historic Garden Week. The local garden club joins in this statewide appreciation of Virginia's springtime splendor. Private homes and gardens are open for public tours. April. Admission charge. Contact the visitor center for information.

Resources

Historic Lexington Foundation
8 E. Washington
Lexington, VA 22456
(703) 463-2552

Historic Lexington Visitor Center
107 E. Washington
Lexington, VA 22456
(703) 463-3777

17

Charlottesville and Albemarle County

Charlottesville and Albemarle County are known as "Jefferson's country." This is not a grandiose assumption or advertising slogan. Our third president truly loved this land he chose for his home. His work is reverently preserved throughout the area.

Stately Monticello, Jefferson's estate, sits atop the little mountain for which it was named and seems to contemplate the city below. The University of Virginia, which he conceived and built, was one of Jefferson's proudest achievements. Several other homes in the county, including James Monroe's plantation, Ash Lawn, were also designed by Jefferson.

Today city planners, residents, and the University community take the standards and ideals he set out very seriously. In fact, Mr. Jefferson (as he is respectfully referred to in Charlottesville) is mentioned so frequently, you'd think he was still in residence on the mountain.

Several national publications have included Charlottesville in their lists of the "top ten places to live" when measuring "quality of life." Because of its care in preserving historic areas and guidance in overseeing modern development, Charlottesville has twice been named an "All-American City."

Charlottesville and South–Central Areas

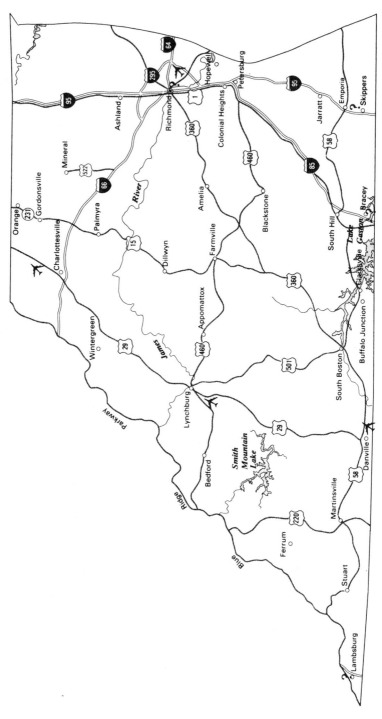

History

Initially, the county which now surrounds Charlottesville was formed in 1744 and named for the governor-general of the colony, William A. Keppel, second Earl of Albemarle. While this region was mostly wilderness, Jamestown to the east had been a bustling community for over a century. Through the years, the boundaries of Albemarle were to shift because of misinterpretation of standing landmarks. This often resulted in the use of local lore for legal divisions. For example, one property line was identified as "running up to the head of the branch that the Indian shot John Lawson at."

In 1761, a 1000-acre tract was purchased from Richard Randolph of the Richmond area. A courthouse square was built and in 1762 the General Assembly established the town of Charlottesville and named it for Queen Charlotte, wife of George III. Land lots were sold rapidly, and shops, taverns, and residences sprang up within the town.

Many well-known adventurers, patriots, and founding fathers of our country were born in this newly established community. George Rogers Clark, revolutionary soldier, and Meriwether Lewis, explorer of the Western territories, had homes in the county. Thomas Jefferson built his cherished Monticello just several miles to the east of the city. It stands as a classic structure in American architecture. From its vantage point, looking out across the foothills to the Blue Ridge mountains, Mr. Jefferson was inspired to build the University of Virginia, the passion of his later years. James Monroe, our fifth president, had a residence constructed adjacent to Monticello. He wanted to be close to his dear friend who had the desire to create "a society to our taste." The home was designed by Jefferson and is a fine example of a nineteenth century working plantation. An abnormally low arch that leads to the gardens facing his friend's estate created a standing joke between the two men. Whenever Monroe used this walkway, he was teased that he was actually bowing in deference to the Jefferson home.

The onset of the Revolutionary War produced a history which is rich in tales about Charlottesville's patriots. A favorite is the story of Jefferson's escape to Staunton from Tarleton's raid on Monticello. The British general's strategy was to capture key leaders in the colonies' struggle for independence and remove them to England. However, Jack Jouett, the lesser known Revere-like hero, heard of the plan and raced on horseback to warn the patriots and allow for an eleventh hour escape.

With the exception of Tarleton's raid, Charlottesville was not greatly affected during the War for Independence. The internment of four thousand British soldiers and Hessian mercenaries captured after General Burgoyne's defeat at Saratoga caused some excitement, but, more importantly, it created a financial boom for the city. The necessity of feeding, clothing, and housing the prisoners provided welcome relief from the disabled war economy. A number of these inmates escaped and ran off to the hills in the west. Today local residents of these mountain communities still bear names of the early English prisoners.

After the war, clearance of the nearby Rivanna River assisted in further boosting the economy. Jefferson considered the completion of this task one of his greatest achievements. It made possible the transportation of goods and constituted a main avenue for traffic until the railroads came through in 1848.

A woolen mill, built near the river, emerged as the area's first industry in the 1830s. It was razed by Sheridan during the Civil War since it produced the fabric which clothed Confederate soldiers. The mill was later rebuilt and during its years of production stood as a symbol of the Reconstruction as well as an example of the many advantages that the city could provide to prospective factories.

Throughout the years, Charlottesville has maintained her strength in industry and the agricultural trades while developing into the surrounding area's commercial marketing center. The university has grown from the small "Academical Village" into one of this nation's finest institutions of higher learning. Although housing developments, new shopping centers, and fast food restaurants have encircled the original town and continue to creep into the countryside, the city is resolute in maintaining the dignity of her historical center.

Places to Visit/Things to Do

Ash Lawn (2½ miles past Monticello, on SR 795). The home of James Monroe was originally called the Highlands. Designed by Thomas Jefferson, this eighteenth century plantation is only about two miles from Monticello. The two men had long wished to live near each other in order to enjoy their strong friendship. Ash Lawn offers tours of the home and grounds. Peacocks sit beneath pear trees, and visitors are encouraged to enjoy the gardens by picnicking or just relaxing. Throughout the year a full schedule of special events is planned (see under **Seasonal Events**). Open daily 9 to 5 November through February, 9 to 6 March through October. Closed Christmas Day. Admission charge. Phone (804) 293-9539.

City Market (Charlottesville). From June to October farmers and crafters offer their products to the public. Home-grown apples, tomatoes and greens, fresh-baked breads and pies, aprons, bonnets, and knitted goods are sold. Browsing through the stands gives visitors a perfect opportunity to meet Charlottesvillians and sample their wares. Every Saturday, some weekdays. Check with the Chamber of Commerce for specific dates and location. Free.

The Rotunda at the University of Virginia, designed by Thomas Jefferson

Court Square (East Jefferson Street, downtown Charlottesville). The Albemarle County Courthouse and the surrounding historical buildings are as lively today as they were in the 1700s. The early residents of the newly established town of Charlottesville grew accustomed to the sight of presidents Jefferson, Madison, and Monroe visiting on the Square lawn. During the Revolutionary War, the courthouse protected the Virginia Assembly from the British General Cornwallis and his men. Today, lawyers, realtors, and other professionals occupy the old buildings. A walking tour and other information are available at the courthouse. Free.

Fan Mountain Observatory (U.S. 29 South). One of the largest observatories on the East Coast, Fan Mountain Observatory is open to the general public only once a year. The formal presentation and viewing through the huge telescope are enhanced by local amateur astronomers who set up their scopes on the grounds and invite passers-by to take a gaze at the heavens. Usually held in late April. Free. For information on dates call the Newcomb Hall Information Desk at the

University of Virginia, (804) 924-3601. For information about special programs, phone 924-7494.

Local Theatre. Act I, Four County Players, and the Charlottesville Light Opera Company are just a sample of the local community dramatic groups. Check the local papers for upcoming productions.

McCormick Observatory (University of Virginia). Though smaller and less sophisticated than Fan Mountain, this old observatory is much more accessible. Twice a month astronomy students offer programs and descriptions of celestial bodies observed through the telescope. Free. Call the Newcomb Hall Information Desk of the university, (804) 924-3601.

McGuffey Art Center (201 2nd Street, Charlottesville). Local artists lease studio space in this beautiful old schoolhouse. In exchange for reduced rents to the tenants, visitors are allowed to stroll through the workrooms and watch the artists at work. The gallery space on the first floor is used for exhibits by local or visiting artists. Dance, mime, painting, pottery, stained glass, and quiltmaking are just some of the arts practiced at McGuffey. Check for the Brown Bag Lunch Artist Lecture series and other special events. Open 10 to 5 Tuesday through Saturday, 1 to 5 Sunday. Closed Mondays, Thanksgiving and Christmas. Free. Phone 295-7973.

Second Street Art Gallery. Located in the McGuffey Center, at this gallery contemporary work by regional and nationally known artists is on exhibit. Open as McGuffey Center. Free.

Historic Michie Tavern (VA 53, between Charlottesville and Monticello). Historic Michie Tavern is just down the mountain from Monticello and Ash Lawn. Only the New York Metropolitan Museum of Art has a collection that compares with the preRevolutionary furniture and artifacts on display. After touring the exhibits and grounds, enjoy a meal the way Jefferson, Madison, and Monroe did in The Ordinary. Colonial dining daily, from 11:30 to 3:00 (See also **Dining**). Phone (804) 977-1234. Admission Charge.

Monticello, home of Thomas Jefferson

Monticello (2 miles southeast of Charlottesville, on VA 53). The magnificent estate of former President Thomas Jefferson lies just outside the city limits overlooking Charlottesville and the Blue Ridge Mountains. Styled like a classic hilltop Greek temple, Mr. Jefferson's residence was built and renovated using ideas he brought back from his travels abroad. His final revision was to become one of the most famous buildings in America. Almost everyone unknowingly carries around a picture of this landmark; it is on the back of a nickel. The opportunity to tour the beautiful home and surrounding garden grounds has attracted many visitors to Charlottesville.

The multi-talented Thomas Jefferson was also a creator of many innovations and gadgets. He used his home as a laboratory, and his experimental designs are present everywhere you look. A huge clock that hangs over the main entrance needs winding only once a week. When installed though, it was discovered that either the room was too short or the clock too long. A hole had to be cut in the floor and the last day of the week is noted in the basement. Jefferson also introduced dumbwaiters, self-closing French doors, hidden closets, and copying machines at the mansion.

The gardens of Monticello are filled with bright displays of spring flowers, orderly rows of vegetables, and fragrant herb beds when in season. The terrace leads past the honeymoon cottage where the young Jeffersons spent their first days of marriage. Underground walkways pass the kitchens, wine cellar, and stables. Leaving the house, the path winds downhill to the small cemetery where Jefferson and his family are buried.

Current excavations of the grounds are being carried out by students of the University of Virginia. Some of the unearthed items are on display in the lower quarters. Open daily 9 to 4:30 November through February, 8 to 5 March through October. Admission charge. Phone (804) 979-7346.

Montpelier (Approximately 20 miles northeast of Charlottesville on VA 20). In the neighboring county of Orange, the national Trust for Historic Preservation has opened the doors to the home of James and Dolly Madison. As our 4th President and the "Father of the Constitution," the Madisons entertained family and friends on this 2,700-acre estate. In recent years, the property served as a private residence for the DuPont family and now includes a 55-room mansion, stables, a bowling alley, and the Madisons' Temple and grave. Open daily 10 to 4 except on Thanksgiving, Christmas, and New Year's Day. Admission charge. For information write to P.O. Box 67, Montpelier Station, VA 22957 or call (703) 672-2728 or 672-2206.

University of Virginia (University Avenue, Charlottesville). The Rotunda and Lawn are Thomas Jefferson's original conception of the University of Virginia. These buildings, gardens, and graceful serpentine walls have been called some of the finest examples of American architecture. The "Academical Village" of Jefferson's day includes the stately Rotunda (patterned after the Pantheon), ten pavilions with distinctive architectural styles, and the colonnade of Lawn rooms, which were the original student dormitories.

Behind each pavilion (now occupied by professors) is a small public garden. The designs range from simple gravel paths surrounding fruit trees to more formal layouts of boxwood hedges encircling statues. Visitors often find themselves claiming a bench to enjoy the flowers and the quiet. Garden gates, no two alike, are self-closing, a typical Jeffersonian feature.

The dormitory room of Edgar Allan Poe, once a University of Virginia student, has been preserved. McGuffey's Ash, named for the originator of the primer readers, is the focus of one pavilion garden. Statues of Jefferson and Washington look across the Lawn at each other. It is said that they reach out and shake hands when a pretty woman passes by. Strange symbols and nameplates embellish walks, stairs, and doorways. The students are traditionally friendly in assisting visitors to decipher the meanings of these collegiate hieroglyphics. Tours and information are available at the Rotunda. Free.

The Virginia Players. The University of Virginia Drama Department presents a schedule of nine productions throughout the year. Classic plays, light comedies, and new works by contemporary writers are presented on the Culbreth Theater stage. Also national touring companies performing Broadway plays, dance groups, and musicians often have Charlottesville on their itinerary. Their performances are usually sponsored through the university; information is available at the Newcomb Hall Desk (phone (924-3601) or Theatre Office (phone 924-8966).

Shopping

The Corner (West Main Street, Charlottesville, across from the Univiersity of Virginia chapel and hospital). The original old university neighborhood includes several blocks of small shops and popular restaurants. Expect to find a rare book, fashions for conservative or eccentric moods, and all the University of Virginia souvenirs a "Wahoo" could desire. The Corner is a comfortable, casual place to enjoy a drink at an outdoor cafe.

Crafters Gallery (West of Charlottesville on U.S. 250, 3 miles beyond Ivy). A rustic building deceptively hides a wealth of unusual handmade items including pottery, weavings, and wall hangings. Many of the artists are recognized nationally. Closed on Mondays. Phone 295-7006.

HTG Artworks (301 East Market Street, Charlottesville). National wholesalers of fine handcrafted jewelry, wearables, and small sculptures have a small gallery open to the public off the downtown mall. Limited hours. Call first at 296-3255.

McGuffey Arts Center (201 2nd Street, Charlottesville; see also **Places to Visit.**) The studio gallery exhibits selected items from the artists working in the building. Purchases can be made when the studios are opened for special events. Phone 295-7973.

Paula Lewis Quilt Store (4th and Jefferson streets). This shop features a wide variety of handmade quilts and showpiece antiques. Materials, tools, and accessories are available if the quilts on display inspire an attempt to try your hand at an original. Phone 295-6244.

1740 House Antiques (3 miles west of Charlottesville on U.S. 250). Fine antiques, country primitives, and folk art are displayed in an eighteenth century setting. Phone 977-1740.

Signet Gallery (202 Fifth Street). Shoppers and browsers are invited to enjoy distinctive handcrafted items including woven clothing, original jewelry, and small sculpture. Closed on Mondays. Phone 296-6463.

Dining

The Corner (West Main Street, across from the University of Virginia hospital). This university neighborhood offers many reasonably priced restaurants that tempt passers-by with ethnic cuisine, regional specialties, and vegetarian dishes. Warm weather brings diners onto patios or encourages them to take a "to-go" meal for an impromptu picnic on adjacent university grounds or in the pavilion gardens.

Spudnuts (309 Avon Street). A haven for doughnut lovers. Potato flour is the "secret" spudnut ingredient that brings local fame to this coffee shop. Phone 296-0590.

The Ordinary (Michie Tavern). An authenic colonial midday meal is presented in the converted slave quarters at Michie Tavern. Afternoon visitors to Jefferson's "Little Mountain" can stop in for coffee and cobbler. Phone 977-1235.

C. & O. Restaurant (515 E. Water Street). A warehouse façade masks a simple but elegant dining room upstairs which is recommended throughout the East Coast. Its reputation rests on consistently fine French nouvelle cuisine and impeccable service. Dining in the small pub downstairs can be an equally enjoyable experience. The meals are simpler and less expensive, but reflect the quality upstairs. Phone 971-7044.

Ivy Inn (2244 Old Ivy Road). An attractive Georgian home is the setting for this restaurant. Carefully prepared meals include Southern cooking, seafood and duck dishes, and homemade breads. Phone 977-1222.

Little Johns New York Delicatessen (1427 W. Main Street, on the Corner). New York's thick sandwiches have migrated south. Lox and bagels, cheesecake, and other big city delights. Open 24 hours for early breakfast or late-night snacks. Phone 977-0588.

Terry's Place (119 4th Street N.E.). Come in for breakfast a few times and the staff will probably remember how you like your eggs or if you need cream for your coffee. Open 6:30 A.M. to 3:00 P.M. Phone 296-6509.

Margarita's (1427 W. Main Street, on the Corner). Delicious enchilidas, burritos, soups, and salads can be enjoyed while you look out across the university Lawn. Authentic Mexican flavors (at very reasonable prices) are found surprisingly close to the Jeffersonian columns and traditions. Phone 971-8346.

Timberlake's Drug Store (322 S. Main Street, on the Downtown Mall). Open since 1890. As you walk past the high wooden shelves of the pharmacy to the luncheon counter in the rear, you get the sights and smells of a small town drug store from another age. Simple sandwiches and soups are served for lunch. Here, milk shakes actually mean milk shakes made in a silver fountain mixer. Lunch only. Phone 296-1191.

Virginian (1521 W. Main Street, on the Corner). This casual restaurant has been around since the days when a full-course meal left change from a dollar. Overhead blackboards list the nightly menu, which always includes several vegetarian dishes. Phone 293-2606.

Evening Entertainment

C. & O. (515 E. Water Street). Casual atmosphere. Regional jazz, bluegrass, and rock and roll performers. Small dance floor, full bar. Cover charge. Phone 971-7044.

Court Square Tavern (across from the Albemarle County Courthouse on Jefferson Street). Local pub in historic Court Square. One of the best places in Charlottesville for a drink and conversation. Selection of beers from around the world and full bar. (No live music.) Phone 296-6111.

Millers (109 W. Main Street). Cafe setting in a renovated drugstore. Outdoor patio on downtown mall open during pleasant weather. Small local groups performing. Full bar. Occasional cover charge. Phone 971-8511.

Mine Shaft Cellar (1106 W. Main Street). College student bar and dance setting. Regional and local rock and roll or contemporary groups. Beer and wine. Cover charge. Phone 977-6656.

Lodging

Boar's Head Inn (U.S. 250 W, 2 miles past junction of U.S. 29 and U.S. 250). This resort facility with the charm of a country estate is set in the rolling hills that lead to the Blue Ridge Mountains. Named for the Old English symbol of hospitality, Boar's Head has established a fine reputation throughout the area. A national magazine has listed this Inn among the top fifty tennis resorts in the country. Golf, racquet sports, swimming, and even a hot-air balloon ride can contribute to a memorable stay in Jefferson country. Wine festivals, Dancing Under the Stars, holiday celebrations, and other special events are planned throughout the year. Phone (804) 296-2181.

Oxbridge Inn (316 14th Street NW, Charlottesville). A quaint home offering bed and breakfast. Located in the university area, it is within walking distance of the Rotunda and the Corner. Phone (804) 295-7707.

English Inn of Charlottesville (2000 Morton Drive, Charlottesville). A large Tudor-style inn with eighty-eight bed and breakfast rooms. King-sized suites with a wet bar available. Swimming pool, pub, and dart room. Phone (804) 971-9900.

Guest Houses Bed and Breakfast, Inc. Coordinates a listing of bed and breakfast cottages, private homes, and country estates. It provides a convenient service for travelers weary of traditional motels. A few short-term efficiency apartments are also available. Phone (804) 979-7264 or (804) 979-8327 between 1 P.M. and 6 P.M.

Recreation

Canoeing, Tubing. James River Runners (Scottsville) promises a trip tailored to any taste—from a three-hour float to a four-day cruise. Bring along your own picnic or choose a gourmet lunch or barbeque to be prepared for you on one of the river beaches. Accommodations for a few or several hundred. Phone 286-2338.

Horseback Riding. At Foxfield Stables (Garth Road), English and Western rental horses are available. Ride across 219 scenic acres of western Albemarle County rimmed by the Blue Ridge. Phone 973-4886.

Chris Greene Lake (take U.S. 29 north of Charlottesville, then SR 649 at airport sign; follow signs to lake, on SR 606). Swimming, boating, and windsurfing, a nice sand beach, and a picnic area. Covered picnic area and grills can be reserved. Admission charge. For reservations, call Albemarle County Parks and Recreation, 296-5844.

Mint Springs (take U.S. 250 south of Charlottesville, then VA 240 at sign for Crozet, right onto SR 810 and follow signs). A scenic lake at the foothills of the Blue Ridge Mountains. Covered picnic area and grills can be reserved. Admission charge. For reservations, call Albemarle County Parks and Recreation, 296-5844.

Seasonal Events

Albemarle Harvest Wine Festival (Boar's Head Inn, U.S. 250 W). A promotion and celebration of Virginia wines. Lectures, exhibits, and tastings take place under canopies by the Boar's Head lake. Vineyard tours are available. Admission charge. Phone (804) 296-2181.

Annual Antique Car Show (at Elks Lodge on VA 20 N, ½ mile from intersection of VA 20 N and U.S. 250 E). A fine array of classic automobiles for nostalgia lovers. Sponsored by the

Antique Auto Club of America. First week of May. Phone (804) 295-5202.

Ash Lawn (take VA 20 south from Charlottesville, then left onto VA 53 and follow signs). The original plantation home of James Monroe, our fifth president. Special events include kite day, traditional crafts, exhibits, operas, and outdoor music festivals. Admission charge to some events. Phone (804) 293-9539.

Barracks Road Art Show (Barracks Road Shopping Mall, Emmet Street and Barracks Road, Charlottesville). Painting, sculpture, photography, and drawings are displayed. Held in early May. Free. Phone (804) 977-0100.

Christmas in Charlottesville. Holiday festivities are celebrated in the Colonial and Federal styles in early December and throughout the month. McGuffey Art Center and the local craft fairs offer one-of-a-kind Christmas gifts. Candlelight tours of James Monroe's Ash Lawn and Thomas Jefferson's Monticello are featured. Michie Tavern and Boar's Head Inn offer special holiday feasts. Residents in the historic district open their doors for public tours, and the community celebrates the season with concerts and a University of Virginia *Messiah* "singalong." Admission charge to some events.

Dogwood Festival. Charlottesville and Albemarle County celebrate the flowering of the state tree with two weeks of athletic events, barbecues, fireworks, a carnival, and a parade. April. Admission charge to some events. For information write: Charlottesville Dogwood Festival, P.O. Box 112, Charlottesville, VA 22902.

Foxfield Races (where Barracks Road West becomes Garth Road). For a taste of horse country life, don't miss this steeplechase event. The day begins with a horse and carriage parade. Soon after, the jockeys in their silks are urging the thoroughbreds through jumps on this scenic hill-and-dale course. Spectators are a mix of local picnickers with buckets of chicken and the elegant bunch enjoying tailgate buffets served on china and silver. The races are usually held on the last

Saturday in April and the first Saturday in October. Reserved spaces are available. General admission available the day of the races. For reservations call (804) 293-9501 or 293-8160.

First Night Virginia (416 East Main Street). This special New Year's Eve celebration offers entertainment from belly dancing to big bands to chamber music. The purchase of a "First Night" button allows you to wander in and out of many performances (over 100 to choose from) held during the evening. A citywide parade leads everyone down at midnight for fireworks. Always sold out. Phone (804) 296-8548.

Garden Week. An annual statewide exhibit sponsored by the Virginia Garden Society. In Charlottesville selected historic residences within the university and community are open to the public. The candlelight tour of the university and champagne evening at Ash Lawn are special traditions. Held during the last full week in April. Admission charge.

Greenwood Arts and Crafts Show (in Greenwood, 19 miles west of Charlottesville on U.S. 250 W). Each year a greater number of regional crafters display their works at this event, which is held twice a year in September and December. The outdoor country setting encourages conversations with the artists and an unhurried enjoyment of the individual pieces. While tending their booths, many of the crafters are at work. Admission charge.

Independence Day. Welcome new Americans as they attain their citizenship at the naturalization ceremony at Monticello. The city of Charlottesville also presents concerts, picnics, and family game activities. At the close of day, spread a blanket on the hill, buy an ice cream cone, and lie back to enjoy a colorful fireworks show at McIntyre Park. Admission charge to some events.

Mountain Harvest Festival and Charity Auctions (Crozet). A country auction, square dancing, apple butter-making, and a pig roast are reminiscent of old-time Virginia festivities. Mid-October. Admission charge.

Thanksgiving Hunt Weekend. Two days for horse and hunt

lovers. After the annual Blessing of the Hounds conducted at Grace Episcopal Church (in Cismont), the Keswick Hunt Club welcomes spectators to the start of the foxhunt. The Boar's Head Inn hosts a Thanksgiving feast, a hunt tea, and a foot hunt. Thanksgiving weekend. Admission charge to some events. For information on the Blessing of the Hounds, call Grace Episcopal Church, (804) 293-3549.

Resources

Charlottesville Chamber of Commerce
P.O. Box 1564
Charlottesville, VA 22902
(804) 293-3141
(Located at the corner of East Market and 5th St.)

The Thomas Jefferson Visitors' Bureau
P.O. Box 161
Charlottesville, VA 22902
(804) 293-6789
(Located on VA 20 S, ¼ mile from junction of VA 20 and VA 53 to Monticello.)

18

Highland County

As one leaves the low, rolling hills of the Shenandoah Valley, the sight of Virginia's "Little Switzerland" comes as a rugged contrast. Located on the far side of the Allegheny Mountains, Highland County, at 1630 to 4546 feet, claims the highest mean elevation east of the Mississippi River. The county pockets several mountain villages, where farming and the lumber industry continue to make up a large part of the local economy.

Highland County was settled by two distinct groups: the clans from Great Britain and the Germans. Initially, these new residents lived peacefully with the American natives. At the onset of the French and Indian War, however, Indian attacks began and many pioneers retreated to strongholds east of the Blue Ridge Mountains.

For those who stayed, defense became the major consideration in every facet of life. Homes had to be built with strong timbers, fortressed doors, and few, if any, windows. When barrages were extremely fierce, families fled with their livestock to the safety of a nearby fort.

By the late 1840s these hardy residents had established a solid community and built their own courthouse. This single log cabin became the center of activity for the surrounding woodland homesteads. At the same time in faraway Mexico, Gen. Zachary Taylor was leading a campaign in the Mexican War. His capture of Monterey (meaning kingly mountain) influenced Highland's naming of its new county seat.

Points of Interest

As spring approaches, the maple sap begins to run and Highland County celebrates with its annual *Maple Sugar Festival.* Pancake breakfasts and trout dinners are served at the high school, while the maple sugar camps are open to the public. With Devil's Backbone Mountain in the distance and bluegrass music playing on the courthouse lawn, the craft and antique sellers set up their booths on Main Street in Monterey. The stands selling maple sugar treats (especially the doughnuts) always attract a large crowd. Free.

In the late summer, the changing leaves of the maple tree again signal the time for an annual event. Although the *Highland County Fair* is not as famous as the Maple Sugar Festival, it gives a more intimate glimpse of this rural community. The trip to the fair through the Alleghenies in autumn colors is filled with dips, turns, and valley overlooks, making it one of the prettiest drives in the country. Admission charge.

Monterey is an enchantingly quiet and reclusive place to visit when these seasonal events are not in progress. There are several small shops to browse through, and the courthouse has displays that give additional information about the area. The small, inexpensive restaurants serve daily specials of homecooked meals.

Also found in Monterey is the *Highland Inn* (on U.S. 250 W, 45 minutes from Staunton). It is listed on the Virginia Historic Landmark register, and its restoration has created a charming country environment. The cozy rooms are filled with Victorian antiques and bright quilts, while the small dining room serves some of the regional specialties. Phone (703) 468-2143.

Resources

Highland County Chamber of Commerce
Main Street
Monterey, VA 24465
(703) 468-2550

Bath County

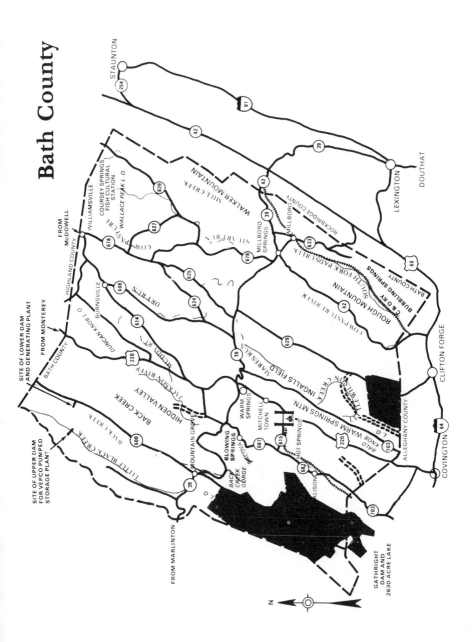

19

Bath County

Bath County, situated at Virginia's western border in the Allegheny Mountains, was originally a common hunting ground for local Indian tribes. The legend claims that an exhausted Indian messenger once paused here to get a drink and discovered a warm spring. After refreshing himself, he slept in the shallow spring bed and awoke rejuvenated. From that time on, the territory served as a neutral ground where any tribe could stop to rest.

These hot springs which continually steam to the surface directed the course of the county's history. By the mid-1700s the first Homestead hotel was built and the resort/spa tradition began. Billiards, dancing, and Irish comedians were included in the entertainment. Tea and dainty tarts were ceremoniously served at five o'clock amidst silver pots. An historian wrote of a Frenchman who didn't know that the way the spoon was placed on the saucer indicated whether more tea was desired. After being overcome by sixteen cups, he simply put the cup and saucer in his pocket to avoid the seventeenth!

Points of Interest

The present-day *Homestead* brings many visitors to the county. Although the price of a meal and lodging is in the expensive range, it is nationally recognized as one of the foremost country resort spas. Travelers to this lovely mountain spot may enjoy three eighteen-hole golf courses, skeet and trap shooting, fishing, indoor pools, bowling, and skiing. Excellent dining in a gracious Southern setting (the kitchen has fifty chefs and bakers) and evening dancing bring many Valley residents across the Alleghenies for a night out. On Sunday afternoons a leisurely brunch can be followed by chamber music, a country walk, or a round of golf. For information write: Homestead, Rt. 220, Hot Springs, VA 24445, or phone (703) 839-5500.

More affordable options for overnight accommodations can be found in approximately ten different motels, inns, and bed and breakfast inns. The Chamber of Commerce makes available a listing of these places in its free brochure, "The County of Bath 1986–87 Visitors Guide."

The town center of Hot Springs has a number of boutiques, specialty shops, and restaurants. Ardent shoppers often travel to the neighboring village of Bacova to make purchases from *The Bacova Guild.* Home items such as mailboxes and icebuckets, all decorated with a rural Virginia motif, are manufactured here. Phone (703) 839-5313.

For music lovers, the *Garth Newel Music Concerts* (on U.S. 220, midway between Hot Springs and Warm Springs) are given on Sunday afternoons in July and August. Admission charge. For information write: Garth Newel Music Center, P.O. Box 427, Hot Springs, VA 24445, or phone (703) 839-5018. Those interested in history can find artifacts of the county and a genealogical library at the *Bath County Historical Society* (Courthouse Square, Warm Springs). Open 9 to 4:30 Monday to Friday, May 1 to November 1. Free. For information write:

Box 212, Warm Springs, Va 24484, or phone (703) 839-2543.

The county is described as the "perfect outdoor playground," and its true treasure is found in the quiet moments spent taking in the hillsides of rhododendron, the rushing streams, and the mountain scenes. *Douthat State Park* and the *George Washington National Forest* are popular recreation sites. The recently built Gathright Dam and Lake Moomaw offer sailing, camping, swimming and picnicking around the 2500-acre lake.

Resources

Bath County Chamber of Commerce
P.O. Box 57
Warm Springs, VA 24484
(703) 839-5409

Appendix

Vineyards

Virginia's young wineries are beginning to earn national recognition. Many varieties of grape now line the rolling slopes of the Shenandoah Valley area. It is wise to phone ahead before planning a visit, as tour schedules vary.

Bacchanal Vineyards
Rt. 2, Box 860
Afton, Va 22960
(804) 272-6937
Directions: Take U.S. 250 W from Charlottesville to VA 6; left on VA 6 for 7 miles (stay on VA 6 when it splits with VA 151); left on SR 631 for approximately 1½ miles.

Barboursville Vineyard
P.O. Box F
Barboursville, VA 22923
(703) 832-3824
Directions: Take VA 20 N from Charlottesville toward Barboursville; turn right on SR 678 for ½ mile to SR 777 (approximately 15 miles from Charlottesville).

LaAbra Farm and Winery
RFD 1, Box 139
Lovingston, VA 22949
(804) 263-5392
Directions: From Charlottesville take U.S. 29 S to Lovingston (approximately 30 miles); then go west on SR 718 4 miles to LaAbra.

Shenandoah Vineyards
Rt. 2, Box 323
Edinburg, VA 22824
(703) 984-8699
Directions: Traveling south on I-81 from Strasburg, take exit
71; turn right at exit ramp; turn right onto SR 686 for 1.5 miles.

Tri-Mountain Winery and Vineyards
Rt. 1, Box 1844
Middletown, VA 22645
Tel. (703) 869-3030
Directions: Located 1 mile from the Middletown exit (exit 77)
on I-81, on VA 627 E.

Two informative brochures listing specific varieties of wine
produced in the area and further details are available from:

"Virginia Vintage"
Virginia Department of Agriculture and Consumer Services
Division of Markets
P.O. Box 1163
Richmond, VA 23209

"Virginia's Wine Country"
Virginia Division of Tourism
202 N. Ninth St., Suite 500
Richmond, VA 23219
(804) 786-4484

Private Campgrounds
(Listed from North to South)

Harpers Ferry KOA. Nature trail, recreation building, store,
swimming, fishing, gas, and laundry. Open April to November 1. Write: Rt. 3, Box 1300, Harpers Ferry, WV 25425. Phone
(304) 535-6895. 1 mile west of park entrance on U.S. 340.

The Cove. Nature trail, swimming, boating, and fishing.

Open daily Memorial Day to Labor Day, weekends only in other months. Gore, VA 22637. Phone (703) 858-2882. From Winchester take U.S. 50 W to Gore; exit on SR 751 to SR 704 for 6 miles.

Battle of Cedar Creek. Store, playground, swimming, boating, fishing, gas, and mini-golf. Open year round. Write: P.O. Box 341, Middletown, VA 22645. Phone (703) 869-1888. Take exit 70 on I-81, North on U.S. 11 for 1 mile.

Fishnet. Nature trail, store, canoeing, fishing, gas, and laundry. Open year round. Write: P.O. Box 1919, Front Royal, VA 22630. Phone (703) 636-2961. Two miles from junction of I-66 and U.S. 522 N; then right onto SR 658 for .7 mile.

Orkney Springs. Recreation building, store, swimming, laundry. Open year round. Write: P.O. Box 1, Orkney Springs, VA 22845. Phone (703) 856-2585. Exit 69 on I-81 to Orkney Post Office (VA 263); then left onto SR 610 for .2 mile.

Skyline Ranch Resort, Inc. Recreation building, store, playground, swimming, fishing, gas, and laundry. Open year round. Write: P.O. Box 393, Front Royal, VA 22630. Phone (703) 636-6061. From Front Royal take U.S. 340 S, then right onto SR 619 for 5 miles.

Rancho. Store, gas, laundry. Open year found. Write: Rt. 1, Box 404, New Market, VA 22844. Phone (703) 740-8313. Follow U.S. 11 South from New Market for 2 miles.

Massanutten Campground, Inc. Recreation building, store, nature trail, playground, swimming, and gas. Open year round. Write: Rt. 3, Box 133-1A, Broadway, VA 22815. Take exit 66 on I-81; then turn right onto U.S. 11 100 yards; then east on SR 608 for 3.2 miles.

Stokesville Park. Store, playground, nature trail, swimming, gas, and laundry. Open May 1 to October 1. Write: c/o H. D. Riddleberger, Rt. 2, Box 125, Mt. Solon, VA 22843. Phone (703) 350-2343. Take VA 42 for 20 miles southwest from Harrisonburg to SR 747; then take SR 730 and follow signs.

Shenandoah KOA. Nature trail, recreation building, store, swimming, boating, fishing, laundry. Open year round. Write:

P.O. Box 95, Verona, VA 24482. Phone (703) 248-2746. Take exit 59 from I-81 and follow signs for 3 miles.

Walnut Hills Campground. Recreation building, store, swimming, fishing, laundry. Open March to October. Write: Rt. 2, Box 387, Staunton, VA 22401. Phone (703) 337-3920. Take exit 55A on I-81; then take SR 608 to U.S. 11; then go south on SR 655 for 2 miles; campground is on left.

Shenandoah Acres. Nature trail, recreation building, store, swimming, laundry, mini-golf. Open year round. Write: P.O. Box 300, Stuarts Draft, VA 24477. Phone (703) 337-1911. On SR 660, 2 miles south of U.S. 340.

Monticello-Skyline Safari. Nature trail, recreation building, store, swimming, fishing, gas, laundry. Open year round. Write: Rt. 1, Box 275, Greenwood, VA 22943. Phone (703) 456-6409. On U.S. 250, ½ mile from exit 10 on I-64.

Lake Reynovia. Nature trail, store, swimming, boating, fishing. Open April 1 to Nov. 15. Write: 1770 Avon St., Extd., Charlottesville, VA 22901. Phone (804) 296-1910. Follow Avon Street from Charlottesville (exit 24 from I-64) for 2.3 miles.

James River Recreation Area. Nature trail, recreation building, store, swimming, boating, fishing, gas, laundry. Open year round. Write: P.O. Box 266, Natural Bridge Station, VA 24579. Phone (703) 291-2727. Take VA 130 across James River to SR 759; then turn left on SR 782 (campground is 3 miles from Natural Bridge and Glasgow).

Public Campgrounds

No reservations unless specified otherwise.

Shenandoah National Park

Big Meadows. Milepost 51.2 on Skyline Drive. Store and laundry. Open March 1 to December 31. Reservations can be made at Ticketron outlets or at the Park.

Lewis Mountain. Milepost 57.5 on Skyline Drive. Store and trails. Open May to October 31.

Loft Mountain. Milepost 79.5 on Skyline Drive. Store, laundry, and trails. May to October 31.

George Washington National Forest

Camp Roosevelt. On SR 675, 8.5 miles northwest of Luray. Fishing. May 22 to September 12.

Elizabeth Furnace. On SR 678; follow VA 55 9 miles southwest of Front Royal. Fishing and hiking. April 1 to December 31.

Hazard Mill. Follow U.S. 340 and SR 613 10 miles southwest of Front Royal; then onto Forest Rd. 236. Fishing and hiking. April 1 to December 1.

Morris Hill. On southern end of Lake Moomaw, 8 miles northwest of Lovingston. Fishing. April 15 to September 30.

North River. On Forest Rd. 95, follow U.S. 250 and SR 715 14 miles northwest of Staunton. Fishing and hunting. Open year round.

Sherando Lake. On SR 664, 14 miles from Waynesboro. Swimming, hiking, and boating. April 1 to October 31.

Todd Lake. 9 miles northwest of Mt. Solon, following SR 731, SR 730, and SR 718. Swimming and fishing. May 15 to December 1.

Blue Ridge Parkway

Otter Creek. Between mileposts 60 and 61. Camping supplies, gas, telephones, trails, fishing, visitor center, naturalist program, and sanitary dumping station. Open year round, weather permitting. Only chemical toilets and frost-free faucets available in winter.

Peaks of Otter. At milepost 86. Camping supplies, gas, telephones, trails, fishing, visitor center, naturalist program, and sanitary dumping station. Open year round.

Roanoke Mountain. Between mileposts 120 and 121. Telephones, trails, naturalist program, and sanitary dumping station. Open year round.

Index